Illustrator
Type Magic

Illustrator
Type Magic

BY GREG SIMSIC

Hayden
Books

Illustrator Type Magic

Library of Congress Catalog Number: 97-78101
ISBN: 1-56830-334-3

Copyright © 1997 Hayden Books

Printed in the United States of America 1 2 3 4 5 6 7 8 9 0

Warning and Disclaimer

Trademark Acknowledgments

President	Richard Swadley
Associate Publisher	John Pierce
Publishing Manager	Laurie Petrycki
Managing Editor	Lisa Wilson
Marketing Manager	Kelli Spencer

The Illustrator Type Magic Team

Acquisitions Editor
Rachel Byers

Development Editor
Beth Millett

Copy/Production Editor
Terrie Deemer

Technical Editor
Gary Adair

Publishing Coordinator
Karen Flowers

Cover Designer
Aren Howell

Book Designer
Gary Adair

Manufacturing
Brook Farling

Production Team Supervisors
Laurie Casey, Joe Millay

Production Team
Trina Brown,
Daniel Caparo,
Wil Cruz,
Diana Groth,
Laure Robinson,
Maureen West

About the Author

Illustrator Type Magic is Greg's latest type effects book. It follows the success of his last two books: *Photoshop Type Magic 1*, co-author, and *Photoshop Type Magic 2*, author. Currently, Greg is a student of sculpture at the Herron School of Art in Indianapolis. He is also 100% not guilty.

Acknowledgments

Once again, thank you Beth and the rest of Hayden for making it easy to put this project together.

Hayden Books

The staff of Hayden Books is committed to bringing you the best computer books. What our readers think of Hayden is important to our ability to serve our customers. If you have any comments, no matter how great or how small, we'd appreciate your taking the time to send us a note.

You can reach Hayden Books at the following:

Hayden Books
201 West 103rd Street
Indianapolis, IN 46290
317-581-3833

Email addresses:

America Online: Hayden Bks
Internet: hayden@hayden.com

Visit the Hayden Books Web site at http://www.hayden.com

Contents at a Glance

Contents

Introduction

I hope that you did not open this book wanting to learn
how to type, because after retyping this line three times
I have decided (admitted) that I know nothing about that
subject. No, what you have here is a compilation of special
effects for creating display type in Adobe Illustrator. All of
the instructions needed to complete each of these 45
effects are contained within separate chapters. I attempted
to include within this book all of the common techniques
for manipulating type—the ones that are used often.
Hopefully, these techniques will either remind you of that
step you forgot, or point out a new method that takes
advantage of Illustrator's lesser-known features and makes
the task a little easier or a little more interesting. Beyond
these standard effects, there are unique treatments that I
came across during countless hours of meandering among
the menus of Illustrator. If you need a little help with some
of Illustrator's basic commands, there is a section titled,
appropriately, "Illustrator Basics," that will show you around
a little. My hope is that you follow these instructions not
only to create what you see on the pages, but to suggest a
new way for you to express your own creativity. The variations included at the end of most effects are just that sort of
thing—they take the preceding instructions and tweak them
just a bit to create a slightly different or vastly different
effect. I hope you enjoy this book, and thank you for picking
it up.

Greg Simsic

Before You Start

You can create virtually anything in Illustrator, but this book shows you how to create the type effects that Illustrator does well, and the ones that you can do without painstaking manipulation.

Although you could skip around through this book and pick up quite a few new Illustrator skills and techniques, I have assumed that you are already familiar with the basic functions of Illustrator's tools. The Pen tool, for example, can be a little confusing, or at the least awkward, to the beginning user. That's where the "Illustrator Basics" section (p.7) comes in. It provides a quick reference for performing basic Illustrator operations. However, the beginner may still need to refer to more detailed instructions like those found in the manual that came with Illustrator.

The type effects in this book have been arranged alphabetically. Often, though, the best effects are created through a combination of techniques. I couldn't resist these combinations, and have tried to cross-reference them when possible (read: when I remembered).

The CD-ROM

Complete with this book, is the *Illustrator Type Magic* CD-ROM. The CD-ROM includes demo software of popular graphics applications, electronic files for many of the type images included in this book, demo versions of third-party plug-ins, and a glorious assortment of fonts for you to enjoy. See Appendix B, "What's on the CD-ROM," for information on accessing all of this great stuff.

New in Illustrator 7.0

Much like the upgrade to Photoshop 4.0, the upgrade to Illustrator 7.0 does less to increase the capabilities of Illustrator than it does to temporarily increase the frustration of long-time users. There are few new capabilities, but considerable reorganization. The experienced user will press a few wrong keyboard shortcuts while working with this new version, but will soon adapt. Menu items have been rearranged. Most significantly many of the features previously included among the Filter menus and submenus have been relocated to other menus. Although the new organization makes sense, you may miss the fact that some of these features no longer enjoy the convenience of a repeat feature. Add Anchor Points, a command often applied more than once consecutively, is probably the biggest loser in this regard. Perhaps, the most significant new feature for those concerned with type is the addition of the Vertical Type tool. You could always run type in any direction, but now you can stack type on a path. See page 18 for a little information on this new tool.

Illustrator 6.0

Only a few effects in this book cannot be created with Illustrator 6.0. Users of version 6.0 will only have to do a little translation to perform the tasks outlined in the steps. Some items are in different menus, some keyboard commands have changed, but most commands are very similar to Illustrator 6's. The greatest difference affecting the techniques in this book are the way that color attributes are handled. Keep an eye on the screen captures and you'll be able to keep up easily.

Windows Users

With the release of Illustrator 7.0, Macintosh and Windows users are using an almost identical application.

Windows users who are upgrading will find significant improvements over the last version—the Pathfinder utilities are now included, multiple levels of Undo are available, color separations are built-in, and Illustrator for Windows will accept all Photoshop-compatible plug-in filters.

System Setup

Macintosh

The Adobe Illustrator 7.0 information box displays a suggested RAM allocation of approximately 15MB. It will not run with less than 11MB. Although Illustrator is not as much of a memory hog as raster graphics applications such as Photoshop, you may still prefer to raise the Preferred size to 20 or 30MB if you can afford to. Illustrator can use this extra memory if you are using some of the more memory-intensive features, including many, many gradients—the "Petals" and "Shaggy" thumbtabs are good examples of this.

Windows

Adobe recommends an Intel 486 processor with Windows 95 or Windows NT 4.0, 16MB of RAM and 25MB of space available on the hard drive. Although Illustrator is not as much of a memory hog as raster graphics applications such as Photoshop, you should allocate as much RAM as you can to the application. Illustrator can use this extra memory if you are using some of the more memory-intensive features, including many, many gradients—the "Petals" and "Shaggy" thumbtabs are good examples of this.

Third–Party Plug-ins

Almost all of the techniques in this book can be created without the use of third-party plug-ins. However, when it was particularly useful or particularly tempting I did sneak them in. They are more commonly used in the Variations. If a filter was used to create an effect or one of its variations then it is included in the Toolbox. The "Filters" section (page 64) includes additional information on effects that can be achieved directly with these filters. Also, check out the CD-ROM, which includes demo versions of all of these filters.

Conventions Used in This Book

The Blue Type

Take a look at the steps for one of the techniques and you will notice that occasionally a few words are printed in light blue. The color indicates that there is additional information for performing this operation in the "Basics" section on page 7. These are typically basic Illustrator operations. Rather than clutter the steps with information that the familiar user already has hammered into his head, the beginning user is referred to the "Basics" section for a little brush-up. The advanced user will understand these commands and be able to perform them as normal and move through the technique.

The Toolbox

The Toolbox is located below the thumbtab on the first page of each technique. It lists all third-party plug-ins needed to create the type effect or one of its variations.

The Type Tool

This book is all about type, so you will be using the Type tools often. Unless instructed otherwise, use the normal Type tool to enter the text. I have only used the Area Type tool, Path Type tool, and Vertical Type tools in special situations.

Point Size and Scale

Illustrator enables you to scale objects at will without losing quality. For this reason, I suggest that for most of the techniques you work at a scale similar to that used in the book. Most of the type treatments use type that is in the neighborhood of 100 points. When finished with the effect you can use the Scale tool, discussed in the "Basics" section on page 7, to set the type to the appropriate size for your specific use. Remember to turn on the Scale Line Weight option in the Scale dialog box or in the General Preferences (File➡Preferences➡General) so that the strokes are also scaled with the type.

Menu Commands

Throughout the steps you will find instructions such as these:

Choose Filter➡Distort➡Roughen (Size: 3%, Detail: 10/in, Points: Corner)

This example asks you to apply the Roughen filter to the current selection. To perform this command use the mouse to click on the Filter menu at the top of the screen, and then drag down to Distort. When Distort is highlighted, a new menu pops out to the right. Move down this list to Roughen and release the mouse.

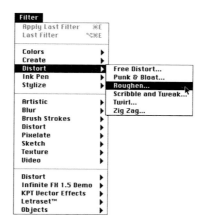

5

In this example a dialog box opens. Enter the information that follows the command in parentheses into the appropriate fields in the dialog box. This dialog box also has a Preview option that enables you to preview the effect of the filter. Many dialog boxes now have preview options, which are a great help when searching for the right settings.

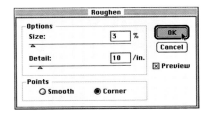

If there is no parenthetical information following a command, then either the command has no variable settings or the proper settings are discussed elsewhere in that step. Click OK to roughen the type.

Within the instructions, Macintosh keyboard shortcuts, sometimes set off by parentheses, are followed by the Windows keyboard shortcuts set off by brackets.

Settings

Regard the settings that are used in the steps as guides. If you are using a similar typeface at a similar point size, then you will probably be able to use the same settings that are included in the steps. Otherwise, you may need to adjust the settings to the needs of your type. The best rule is to keep an eye on the illustrations and make sure that your type continues to resemble my example. See "Point Size and Scale" for more information on this topic.

Tips

Tips are scattered throughout the book as helpful hints for working through the steps. They may provide a little extra information to get you through the instructions if you're having trouble. Or, they may contain information about improving an effect.

Illustrator Basics

The descriptions contained on the following pages are intended to help the novice get through some of Illustrator's routine tasks. The titles correspond to the blue text in the type effects instructions.

Illustrator also has an online manual that you can find under the Balloon menu while in Illustrator. It contains some good general information on Illustrator basics.

The Toolbar

You can access tools by either clicking them on the Toolbar (see illustration) or pressing the letter that corresponds to that tool. For tools that are contained within pop-out menus of the Toolbar, pressing the letter shortcut will cycle through the tools in that menu. Many of the tools have settings which can be changed in their dialog boxes. To access the dialog box for a tool, double-click on the tool.

Press (Command)[Control] while using any tool to access the current selection tool. If the current selection tool is the Direct Selection tool or the Group Selection tool, then pressing the (Option)[Alt] key while holding down the (Command)[Control] key will toggle between these two tools.

(Command-Tab)[Control-Tab] toggles between the normal Selection tool and the Direct Selection tool or Group Selection tool, whichever one is the current tool in that submenu.

This illustration of the Toolbar displays the common names assigned to each tool. The tools will be referred to by these names.

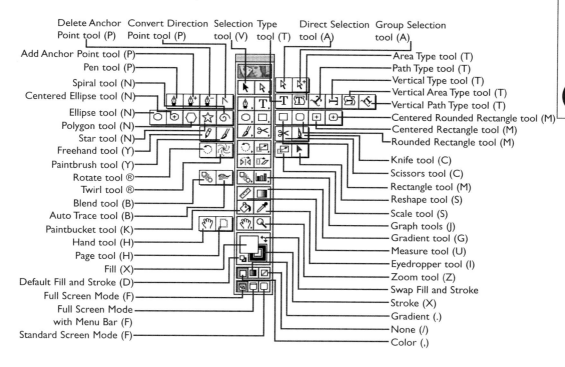

7

Accessing Palettes

To display any palette, except the Character, Paragraph and MM Design palettes, that is not currently onscreen, click the Window menu and scroll down to the palette you want to display. The Character, Paragraph, and MM Design palettes are accessed through the Type menu. To close a palette click the close window icon in the top-left corner of each palette.

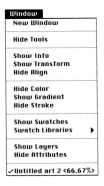

Tips to Make Life Easier

Hide Edges/Show Edges

Shortcut: (Command-H)[Control-H] toggles the edges on and off

The edges that show you what object, paths, or points are selected can sometimes get in the way of seeing what you're trying to do, or what you've done. To temporarily turn off the edges, press (Command-H)[Control-H]. Press it again to turn them back on.

Hide Objects/Show Objects

Shortcut: (Command-U)[Control-U] / (Command-Shift-U)[Control-Shift-U]

Objects can get in the way too. To hide an object, select it and press (Command-U) [Control-U]. To reveal all hidden objects press (Command-Shift-U)[Control-Shift-U]. After revealing the hidden objects, they will all be selected. Also, an object that is hidden cannot be selected until it is revealed.

Lock Objects/Unlock Objects

Shortcut: (Command-L)[Control-L] / (Command-Shift-L)[Control-Shift-L]

A locked object cannot be selected, but is still visible. Select the object and Press (Command-L)[Control-L] to lock it. It will appear as if Illustrator is just ignoring it. If you need to select an object that is being completed covered by another, lock the top object, and you will be able to easily select the object beneath it. Press (Command-Shift-L) [Control-Shift-L] to unlock all objects and select them.

A Few Shortcuts:

(Command-+)[Control-+] zooms in.

(Command--)[Control--] zooms out.

(Command-Spacebar)[Control-Spacebar] to access the Zoom in tool at any time.

(Command-Option-Spacebar)[Control-Alt-Spacebar] to access the Zoom out tool at any time.

Press the Tab key to hide all palettes. Press it again to reveal them.

Spacebar accesses the Hand tool at any time, except while typing.

The Basics

Change the Type Attributes

Type attributes include Font, Point Size, Leading, Kerning, Tracking, Horizontal Scale, Vertical Scale, and Baseline Shift. They can be changed if the type is selected with a Type tool or a Selection tool. Once the type is selected, all attributes can be changed on the Character palette. Press (Command-T)[Control-T] to access the Character palette.

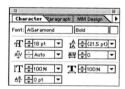

Create Outlines

In order to create many of the effects in this book, the type must be converted to outlines. To do this choose Type➡Create Outlines. This command changes the shapes of the type into paths. The type will look as though it thickens slightly, but there is normally little to no change in the actual type.

Place an Image

You can place raster graphics files in Illustrator with the Place command. These images can then be manipulated and used as elements of type effects such as "Masked," "Rasterized," and "Overlapped." To place an image choose File➡Place.

9

Illustrator Type Magic

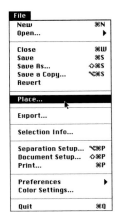

A dialog box opens. Find the file to place.

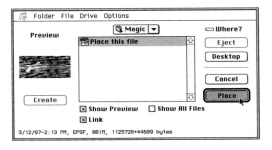

Save the File

To save a file, choose File➡Save As.

A dialog box appears, requesting you to name the document, determine where you want to save it, and choose a file type.

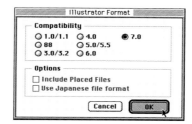

Another dialog box will open. Choose a version of Illustrator in which to save the file, and click OK.

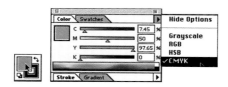

Set the Fill Color

Click the Fill icon on the Toolbar to activate it, and then find the Color palette. The pop-up arrow menu on the color palette allows you to choose from Grayscale, RGB, HSB, and CMYK color modes. Move the pointer over the color strip at the bottom of the Color palette. The arrow will become an Eyedropper and allow you to select a color by clicking on it. You can also enter the values from the keyboard.

Alternately, you can access the Swatches palette after activating the Fill icon. There are five buttons at the bottom of the palette. Click on each to access the swatches within that group.

Set the Stroke Color

Click on the Stroke icon on the Toolbar to activate it. Then use the Color and Swatches palettes as described in the "Set the Fill Colors" section.

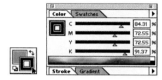

Set the Stroke Weight

Click the Stroke icon on the Toolbar to activate it, then find the Stroke palette to change the settings.

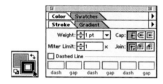

Shift-Select

To add an object to the already selected objects, hold the Shift key while clicking on the new item. All Selection tools have this functionality. The same method will deselect an object from the group of objects selected.

Use the Blend Tool

The Blend tool allows you to create intermediary objects that show the progress of one object transforming into another. Select two objects. Then select the Blend tool. Click once on a point on the path of the first object. A dash will appear below the crosshairs. Click on a point on the path of the second object. The specific points chosen will have a great effect on the final results. For subtle transformations, choose two points that are on similar parts of the objects. A dialog box opens. The number of steps indicates the number of objects that will be created between the two objects.

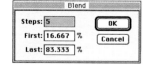
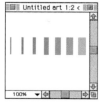

Use the Ellipse/Rectangle Tool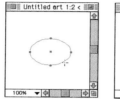

The Ellipse tool and Rectangle tool work by clicking in the image area and dragging the pointer to create a shape. Holding the Shift key while dragging constrains ellipses to circles and rectangles to squares. Holding the Option key while dragging will center the ellipses and rectangles around the point that was clicked.

To create a shape of exact dimensions, click the tool once in the image area to open a dialog box in which you can enter the specifications for the shape. If you hold the (Option)[Alt] key as you click in the image area, then the point that you click will become the center point for the shape.

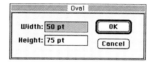

Use the Pencil Tool

The Pencil tool enables you to use the mouse like a pencil. Simply click and drag. To set the Curve Fitting Tolerance, the amount that Illustrator will deviate from the precise movements of the mouse in order to create a smoother line, choose File➡ Preferences➡General. The default is 2 pixels and is a good general setting.

Use the Gradient Tool

This tool is used only for changing the *direction* of a gradient within a path or group of paths. Creating gradients is discussed in the "Gradients" technique on page 76. To redirect a gradient, select an object filled with a gradient, and select the Gradient Tool. Click the crosshairs at the point you want the gradient to start and drag to the point you want the gradient to end. Areas in the path that come before the beginning point will be filled with the color that begins the gradient. Areas that follow the end point of the drag will be filled with the color that ends the gradient. You can also change the direction of the gradient by selecting the filled object and changing the Angle on the Gradient palette.

Use the Paintbrush Tool

The Paintbrush tool works the same as the Freehand tool, except the Paintbrush creates filled paths instead of path lines. Double-click the icon on the Toolbar to open the Paintbrush Options dialog box. The variable width option can only be used if you have a pressure-sensitive tablet.

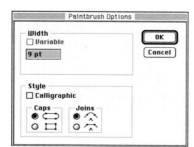

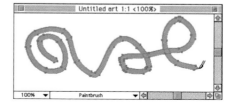

14

Use the Pen Tool

For most beginners, this tool is the most confusing tool. However, you've got to take it on because you are going to use it often in Illustrator. Essentially, the pen tool enables you to create paths—a series of points linked by curves that connect them. I'll walk you through the construction of a simple line.

Select the Pen tool and click once in the image area to create the first point. Then move away from that point and click the pen tool again to create the second point. As you click hold the mouse button down and drag the Pen tool (now a black pointer) in any direction. Watch as the curve bends and twists. Release the mouse button and you've got a line and the basics of the Pen tool. Move the Pen tool directly over the original point. A small circle appears below and to the right of the Pen tool. This circle tells you that clicking on the point will close the path. Click on the point to close path.

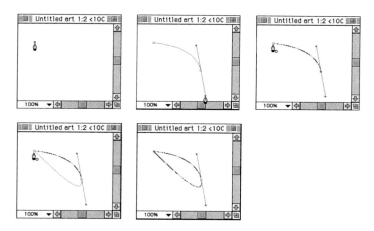

There are other modes of the Pen tool, as well as three other tools that are used in conjunction with the Pen tool:

Hold down the (Option)[Alt] key to access the Convert Direction Point Tool

Hold down the (Command)[Control] key to access the current selection tool

Hold down the Shift key to constrain the paths to true horizontal, vertical, and 45° lines.

The Add Anchor Point tool adds an anchor point to an existing path

The Delete Anchor Point tool deletes an anchor point from an existing path

Use the Convert Direction Point tool to click on a point and drag to change the direction of the paths coming into the point.

Use the Selection Tool

Illustrator contains three selection tools: the Selection tool, the Group Selection tool, and the Direct Selection tool. You will use all of them in this book.

The Selection tool selects entire objects, entire groups of object, and entire compound paths.

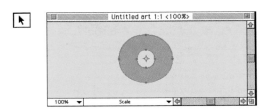

The Direct Selection tool selects single points and single segments of paths.

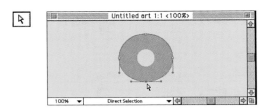

The Group Selection tool selects a single path within a grouped path or a single path within a compound path. Pressing it a second time on the same path will select all paths in the first level of grouping. If you continue to press it, it will select all paths within the next level until all paths at all levels of a group are selected.

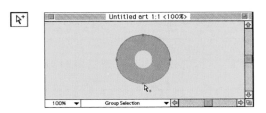

Use the Transformation Tools

The Shear, Scale, Reflect, and Rotate and Twirl tools all have the capability to transform type, and they all work just about the same. For each, the first step is to click once in the image area to set the orientation point around which the operation will take place. The crosshairs will turn into an arrow. Then simply click the pointer and drag it to transform the object.

16

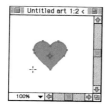  

If you hold down the Option key as you click for the orientation point, a dialog box will open in which you can set the transformation numerically. If you double-click the icon on the Tool palette for any of these tools except the Twirl, a dialog box will open directly. You must set an orientation point before using the Twirl tool.

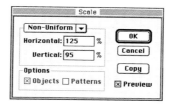

Use the Type Tool

There are six Type tools in Illustrator. If not otherwise specified in the instructions, use the normal Type tool.

Type Tool   [T]

There are two ways to use this tool:

1. Click in the image area. A point will be placed and a blinking cursor will appear. You're ready to type. This is the normal method for entering type in this book.

2. Click in the image area and drag to create a text box. As you type the text will be contained within this box. Also, use this tool to select type as text. Use the Selection tool to select type as objects.

17

Illustrator Type Magic

Area-Type Tool

Click on a path to transform the object into a text box. A blinking cursor will appear within the path, and as you type, the text will be contained within the path.

Path-Type Tool

Click on a path to transform the path into a guide for the type. As you type, the type will follow the line of the path.

Vertical Type Tools

The Vertical Type tools (Vertical Type tool, Vertical Path Type tool, Vertical Area Type tool) function the same as the normal Type tools, except that the letters are stacked on top of each other instead of being placed next to each other.

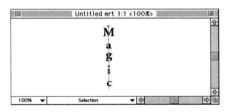

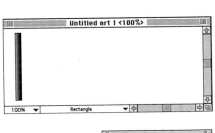

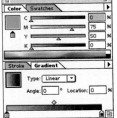

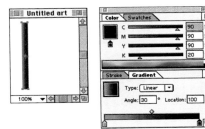

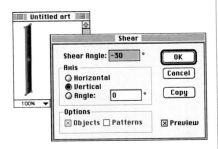

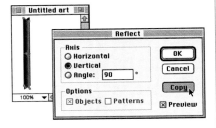

This illusion is created by manipulating the type with the Shear tool.

1 Use the Rectangle tool to create the first baffle of the curtain. This rectangle is 11×130 points. Set the fill color of the rectangle to the Black, White gradient. Set the stroke color to black.

2 Click the fill color icon on the Toolbar to activate it, then find the Gradient palette. Click the white color stop under the gradient. Choose a new color from the Color or Swatches palette (CMYK: 0, 75, 50, 0). The color will show up in the gradient on the Gradient palette and in the baffle.

3 Click on the black color stop under the gradient at the far right. Activate the Color palette and choose CMYK from the arrow pop-up menu. Adding color to the black will help create a better gradient. Set the C, M, and Y values to 90%. Set the K value to 20%.

4 Keep the baffle selected, and double-click the Shear tool to open the Shear dialog box. Set the Axis to Vertical and the Shear Angle to −30° Click OK to shear the baffle.

5 Double-click the Reflect tool to open the Reflect dialog box. Set the Axis to Vertical. Click Copy to create a mirrored copy of the baffle.

6 Use the Selection tool to align the baffles as shown in this figure.

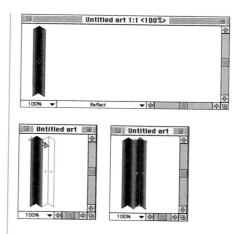

7 Select both baffles. Then, while holding down the Shift and (Option)[Alt] keys, click the upper-left corner of the original baffle with the Selection tool and drag it to the right until the pointer is directly over the upper-right corner of the mirrored baffle. Two copies of the baffles should be aligned as shown here.

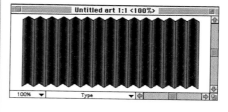

8 Press (Command-D)[Control-D] as many times as it takes to create a curtain long enough to contain the type. Select all of the baffles and press (Command-L)[Control-L] to lock the baffles.

9 Use the Type tool to enter the text (I used Humanist521BT ExtraBold, 90 points). Set the Horizontal Scaling to 67%. Because the type is being squeezed, this scaling will help create the illusion that the type recedes along the direction of the baffles. Choose Type➡Create Outlines. Press (Command-8)[Control-8] to turn the type into a single compound path. Position the type over the curtain.

10 Press (Command-Shift-L) [Control-Shift-L] to unlock and select the curtain. Copy it, and paste a copy in front (Command-F) [Control-F]. Shift-select the type. Choose Object➡Pathfinder➡Crop. Press (Command-Shift-G)[Control-Shift-G] to ungroup the cropped

baffles. The curtain gradient will fill the striped type. The stroke color will change to none.

11 To set the stroke color back to black, select the Eyedropper tool while the type is still selected and double-click on one of the pieces of the curtain. The Eyedropper tool will apply the color attributes of the curtain to the type.

12 Select the individual pieces of type contained within a single column. For columns containing more than one piece, you can Shift-select all pieces in the column.

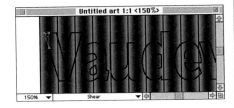

13 Double-click the Shear tool. Set the Axis to Vertical and the Shear Angle to 30° or −30° depending on which column of type is selected. The type should match the Shear Angle of the baffles. Turn on the Preview option to make sure the angle is correct, then click OK.

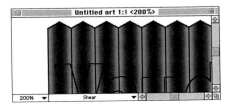

14 Repeat this step for each column. The Shear Angle will alternate between 30° and −30°. Keep the Axis at Vertical.

15 Finally, to change the color of the type, select all pieces of type that fall within every other column.

16 Then click the Fill icon on the Toolbar to activate it. Find the Gradient palette. Click the left color stop under the gradient—the one that isn't black. Choose a new color from the Color or Swatches palette (CMYK: 55, 0, 65, 0). The color will show up in the gradient on the Gradient palette and in the type.

17 Select all of the other pieces of type and change the gradient stop color. ■

23

Antiquing

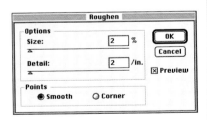

Use the Roughen filter to add some wear to that crisp, clean digital type.

1 Use the Type tool to enter the text. I used Albertus at 85 points. Choose Type➥Create Outlines.

2 Choose Object➥Path➥Add Anchor Points. This feature adds new points along the type outline paths. To be precise, it adds one new point between each pair of existing points, nearly doubling the number of points on the path. The additional points will give the Roughen filter more places to distort the type. Repeat this command about four more times. You should have so many points that they turn into one big blob around the edges of the type. Press (Command-H) [Control-H] to hide the blob, but keep the type selected.

> **TIP** **Be careful not to add too many points because it causes the paths to become more complex, which may cause preview and printing problems later.**

3 Choose Filter➥Distort➥ Roughen. The Roughen dialog box will open with a few settings you can play with. To create this subtle technique, it's best to keep the settings low. Try these settings: Size: 2; Detail: 2, Points: Smooth. Take advantage of the Preview option to see what effect the Roughen filter will have. The distortion can be as fine or as rough as you like. Use this dialog box to control the look of the type.

4 Click OK and you're done.

 If you don't like what you came up with, then press (Command-Z)[Control-Z] and (Command-Option-E) [Control-Alt-E] to restore the type and bring back the Roughen dialog box.

VARIATIONS

A Smoother Version

In Step 2, apply the Add Anchor Points feature once. In Step 3, use these settings in the Roughen dialog box: Size: 2, Detail: 1, Points: Smooth. Changing the Points setting to Smooth will create a smoother effect.

A Rougher Version

Before Step 2, choose Filter→KPT Vector Effects→KPT Shatterbox. Set the Random Lines option high. I raised it to the maximum: 50. This filter will divide the type into many small shards. Set the fill color to black and press (Command-Shift-G) [Control-Shift-G] to ungroup the tiny pieces.

Skip Step 2. In Step 3, try higher settings in the Roughen filter dialog box. I used these: Size: 12, Detail: 10, Smooth. ■

25

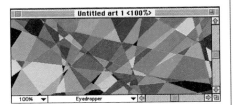

Following are a few techniques for bringing type out of background art.

1 Open a file containing the background art, or create a background to use with the type. I created this background by drawing a rectangle, applying the KPT Vector ShatterBox filter, and the VectorTools Randomize feature on the VectorColor palette. You cannot use a placed image for the background in this effect.

2 Use the Type tool to enter the text. I used 130-point Kabel. Choose Type➡Create Outlines, and Object➡Compound Paths➡Make. Set the stroke color to black and set the stroke weight to 4 points.

3 Select the type and all of the pieces of the background that contact the type (You can select all of the background, as I did, unless you run out of memory). Copy the objects, then paste the copy in front of the originals (Command-F) [Control-F]. You will not see any change onscreen.

4 Choose Object➡Pathfinder➡Crop. The type fill color will disappear.

5 Set the stroke color to black to outline the shapes of the background that lie within the type. Then set the stroke weight to 1 point. The heavy outline set in Step 2 will peak out around the type. Deselect the type (Command-Shift-A)[Control-Shift-A].

VARIATIONS

In Step 2, do not stroke the type. Then skip Step 4, and choose Filter➡Colors➡Saturate. Slide the marker to the left to set the Saturate percentage at −55%.

Again, skip Step 4, and choose Filter➡Colors➡Saturate. This time slide the marker to the right until the type darkens. I set the Saturation at 100%, then reopened the filter dialog box and set the Saturate percentage at 25%.

Instead of completing Step 4, Choose Filter➡Colors➡Invert Colors.

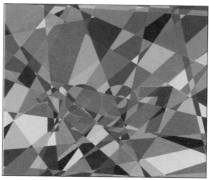

27

Just complete Steps 1 and 2. Don't give the type a stroke, but set the fill color. I used CMYK: 12, 2, 73, 3. Then select the type and background, and choose Object➡Pathfinder➡Soft. Set the Mixing Rate at 50%. This pathfinder will mix the colors of overlapping objects, thus producing a transparent effect.

After Step 4, copy the type (already selected), and paste it in back (Command-B)[Control-B]. Choose Object➡Pathfinder➡Unite. Set the fill color to black. Nothing will have changed onscreen yet. Select the original type (now broken up), and use the arrow keys to move it up and to the left. Copy the type again, and paste it in front (Command-F) [Control-F]. Choose Object➡Pathfinder➡Unite again, then set the stroke color to black.

For this variation, complete Steps 1 through 4, copy the type, and paste it in back (Command-B)[Control-B]. Choose Object➡Pathfinder➡Unite. Set the fill color to white. Then select the original type that was broken up in Step 4. Choose Object➡Transform➡Transform Each. Turn on the Random and Preview options, and set the Horizontal and Vertical Scales both to 50%. Set the Rotate angle at −45°.

Complete Steps 1 through 4, then press (Command-Shift-G)[Control-Shift-G] to ungroup the pieces within the type. Set the stroke color of the pieces to black so you can see the edges. Then select some of the pieces within the type one at a time and set the fill color to black. Do this until the type is as readable as you want it to be. Then choose Edit➞Select➞Same Stroke Color to select all of the type pieces. Set the stroke color to none. Select all of the black type pieces and set the fill color of the pieces to one of the colors from the background. ■

This is a simple trick that uses gradients to create the illusion of a bevel. Illustrator includes special metallic gradients that work well with this technique. See Step 2 to find out how to access them.

1 Enter the text using the Type tool. I used Frutiger Black at 95 points. You will probably need to increase the Tracking in order to make room for the bevel to expand outward. I set the Tracking at 90. Finally, choose Type➡Create Outlines.

2 Fill the type selection with a gradient. Metallic gradients work well with this effect. Illustrator 7 contains extra files of sample gradients that you can access. To access the metallic gradients choose Window➡Swatch Libraries➡Other Library. Then follow this path to find the file: Adobe Illustrator 7.0➡Libraries➡Gradients➡Metals CMYK.ai. The new gradients will open into a new floating palette.

3 I filled the type with this Silver gradient. Use the Gradient tool to direct the gradient across the type from top to bottom. Set the stroke color to none.

4 While the type is still selected, choose Object➡Path➡Offset Path. Set the Offset distance to control how far the bevel spreads away from the letters. For this 95-point type I set the Offset to 4 points (Joins: Miter). Remember, you can use decimals (for example: 3.4) if you need to. The type will look as if it expanded. In fact, the original type outlines still exist. Choose Object➡Pathfinder➡Unite to clean up the odd shapes created at the corners of the type by the Offset Path command. Finally, press (Command-Shift-[)[Control-Shift-[ ] to send the offset type outlines to the back.

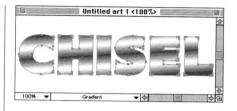

5 The new, expanded type retains the same gradient fill selected in Step 2. Again, use the Gradient tool to direct the gradient angle. Drag across the type in the same direction used in Step 3, but stop the gradient about 3/4 of the way down the type. It's magic: Beveled type!

You will probably have to experiment with the Gradient tool to get the whole thing to work. Gradients that contain a repeating pattern of highlights, like those included in the Metals CMYK.ai file, work best with this effect. Be prepared to redirect the gradient for each individual letter if you are picky.

31

VARIATIONS

Chrome

Try the other gradients in the Metals CMYK.ai file. This effect combines the Silver gradient with the Chrome gradient.

Outline Bevel

For this variation, after completing Step 1, set the fill color for the type to none and give the type a stroke of about 3 pixels (this value sets the width of the outlined letters). Then choose Object➡Path➡ Outline Path after Step 1. Complete the rest of the steps. ▪

Illustrator's Pathfinder feature makes it easy to break up letters into smaller shapes. Following is a technique for crumbling type that allows you to make an endless variety of effects.

The Basic Crumble

1 Use the Type tool to enter the text. I used Helvetica ExtraCompressed at 110 points. Choose Type➡Create Outlines.

2 Break up the text along lines created by the Pencil tool. Deselect the type, then set the fill color to none and set the stroke color to black. Select the Pencil tool and draw many lines across the type. It doesn't matter whether you crisscross the type many times with the same line or draw many separate lines.

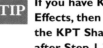

TIP **If you have KPT Vector Effects, then you can use the KPT Shatterbox filter after Step 1. Then skip ahead to Step 7.**

3 Select the line (or all of the lines) and all of the type. Choose Object➡Pathfinder➡Divide. Then choose Object➡Ungroup. Just as you might have guessed, this filter divides the type in to all of the shapes you see created by the line(s). The line(s) will lose its stroke (if it had one), but that's the only change you'll see. Because the fill color of the lines was set to none in Step 2, you won't see anything but the type if the lines are deselected.

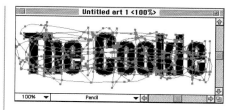

4 Use the Selection tool to select one of the black shapes in the type.

5 Choose Edit➡Select➡Same Fill Color. Copy the pieces, press (Command-A)[Control-A] to select everything and press delete to clear the image. Paste in the black pieces of type. This step will get rid of the extra shapes that were formed around the letters in Step 3 by the Divide filter. The type should be back in place and look like this.

6 Now that the text is split and ungrouped a simple command will crumble it. But first, choose View➡Hide Edges to hide the guidelines.

35

7 Choose Object➡Transform➡ Transform Each. Turn on the Preview and Random options. Then use the pointer to drag the rotation bar around the circle. Watch the preview crumble the type as you try different values. I set the Rotate angle at –51°.

> **TIP** If you don't like what the random feature gave you, click the Preview or Random option off and then on again for a new variation.

8 For a more drastic effect, also slide the Move (Horizontal and Vertical) markers just a little to the left or right. In this example I set the Horizontal Move at 4 points, and the Vertical Move at 2 points.

VARIATIONS

I filled the pieces with two different gradients, and stroked them all with red. Then I copied everything, pasted it in back, chose Object➡ Pathfinder➡Unite, set the fill color of the object to black and shifted it down and to the right to create a shadow.

It may be more effective to crumble only part of the type. Here, I drew lines only at the bottom of the type.

I completed the rest of the previous steps, then used the Selection tool to drag some of the pieces down, away from the type.

Or, copy them as you move them to create a pile of… "alpha-bits"?

I created this striped background.

And placed this crumbled type on top of the background.

I selected the background and the type and chose Object➤ Pathfinder➤Soft. I set the Mixing Rate at 65%. ▪

Illustrator does not come equipped with an easy way to create this effect. But if you have KPT Vector Effects, then you have a filter perfectly suited for this effect—Vector Warp Frame.

1 Use the Type tool to enter the text. I used 100-point Machine. Choose Type➡Create Outlines. Set the Fill and Stroke colors for your type.

2 Choose Filter➡KPT Vector Effects➡KPT Warp Frame. This is a great filter that can do a whole lot more than curve baselines, but we'll stick to that for now. Use the selection arrow to select the lower-left and lower-right corners. (Shift-select to select multiple points, as normal in Illustrator.) Then hold down the Shift key and drag these two points downward.

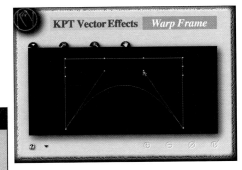

3 Select the two handles that control the upward curve of the baseline. Hold down the Shift key and drag them straight upward until the top of the curve meets the original baseline of the type (indicated by a thin horizontal line). The preview displays exactly what the outlines of your type will look like. When you're satisfied with the distortion, click the check mark in the lower-right corner.

TOOLBOX

KPT Vector
Effects

4 Curved Baselines, Big Deal.

TIP If you want to curve the ends of the type down with less effect on the center part of the type, then choose Double Béziers from the pop-up menu in the upper-left corner of the KPT Warp Frame interface and follow the same steps.

TIP If you have many words that need to be curved, then simply select them one at a time and press (Command-E)[Control-E] to apply KPT Warp Frame with the same settings to each word.

39

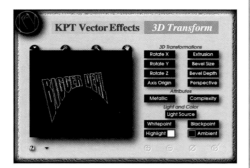

VARIATIONS

Complete Steps 1 through 4, then choose Filter➧KPT Vector Effects➧KPT 3D Transform. More addicting features. Don't worry—you can paint the house tomorrow.

Well worth the lost time.

If you select all four corners in Step 2, and hold down the Option and Shift keys as you move the anchor points, you will create this pinched type effect. ■

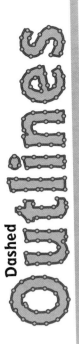

This is a nifty trick that creatively manipulates dashed strokes to produce outline patterns. By layering several copies of type directly on top of each other, each with different stroke settings, you can create an endless variety of patterns that wrap around the oultines of the type. After you've made a few of the patterns shown here, you will soon be making your own.

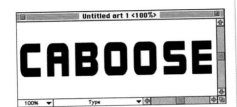

1 Use the Type tool to enter the text. Some of these effects look better with big, blocky fonts, others look better with more curvy, smooth fonts. For the first example I used Bolster Bold at 65 points (Vertical Scale: 150%). I also set the tracking to 150 to make room for the outlines. There is no need to convert the type to outlines, but you can if you want.

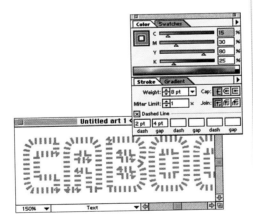

2 Set the stroke color to a brown (CMYK: 15, 30, 80, 25) and set the stroke weight to 8 points. Set the fill color to none. Turn on the Dashed Line option on the Stroke palette. Enter 2 in the first dash slot and 4 in the first gap slot. Select the first icon for both the Cap and Join (Butt Cap, Miter Join).

3 Copy the type, and paste it in front (Command-F)[Control-F]. Turn off the Dashed Line option, and set the stroke weight to 5 points. Change the stroke color to black, and the Join to Round Join.

4 Again, copy the type and paste it in front. Set the stroke color to 50% gray and set the stroke weight to 4 points.

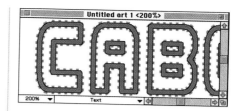

5 Paste in front again. Set the stroke weight to 3 points. This stroke should be black.

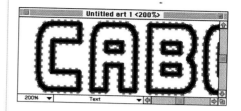

6 Paste in front. Set the stroke color to white and set the stroke weight to 2 points.

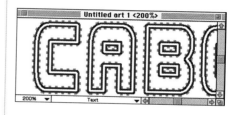

7 Paste in front. Use the same settings as in Step 2, but set the stroke weight to 2 points. All aboard!

Just for your curiosity, here are the six copies of the type separated and in order from bottom to top.

VARIATIONS

To produce these variations, use the settings listed here in place of those used earlier. If the effect is created with layered copies of type, then the First Stroke is the bottom copy. Then each successive copy is pasted in front (Command-F) [Control-F] of the previous one.

43

Snip, Snip

STICKY

GLORY

Cut Along the Dotted Lines

Settings: Badger Bold (85 points); Fill: none; Stroke weight: 3 points; Dash: 8, Gap: 4; Caps: Rounded; Joins: Miter. Copy, paste in back (Command-B)[Control-B] and off-set with the arrow keys to create the shadow. Set the stroke color of the shadow copy to 50% black or any other shadow color you would prefer.

Stamp Edges

Type: Bauhaus Heavy (100 points); Tracking: 100.

First Stroke Settings: Fill: none; Stroke weight: 6 points; Dash: 0.1, Gap: 8; Cap: Round; Join: Round.

Second Stroke Settings: Fill: white; Stroke weight: 3 points; Solid; Cap: Butt; Join: Miter.

Lace

Type: Impact (100 points); Tracking: 75.

First Stroke Settings: Fill: None; Stroke Color: Black; Stroke weight: 8 points; Dash: 0.1, Gap: 8; Cap: Round; Join: Round.

Second Stroke Settings: Fill: None; Stroke Color: White; Stroke weight: 6 points; Dash: 0.1, Gap: 8; Cap: Round; Join: Round.

Third Stroke Settings: Fill: None; Stroke Color: Black; Stroke weight: 4 points; Dash: 0.1, Gap: 8; Cap: Round; Join: Round.

Fourth Stroke Settings: Fill: None; Stroke Color: White; Stroke weight: 2 points; Dash: 0.1, Gap: 8; Cap: Round; Join: Round.

Fifth Stroke Settings: Fill: White; Stroke Color: Black; Stroke weight: 0.5 points; Solid; Cap: Butt; Join: Miter.

Mumps

Type: Garamond Bold, 90 points.

First Stroke Settings: Fill: none; Stroke Color: Black; Stroke weight: 2 points; Solid; Cap: Butt; Join: Miter.

Second Stroke Settings: Fill: none; Stroke Color: Black; Stroke weight: 5 points; Dash: 0.1, Gap: 15; Cap: Round; Join: Round.

Third Stroke Settings: Fill: none; Stroke Color: CMYK: 37, 0, 57, 0; Stroke weight: 3 points; Dash: 0.1, Gap: 15; Cap: Round; Join: Round.

Fourth Stroke Settings: Fill: CMYK: 37, 0, 57, 0; Stroke Color: None.

Lines

Type: Gando, 120 points, Tracking +90.

First Stroke Settings (optional Shadow): Fill: none; Stroke Color: Black; Stroke weight: 5 points; Dash: 0.1, Gap: 4; Cap: Butt; Join: Miter.

Second Stroke Settings: Fill: none; Stroke Color: CMYK: 35, 10, 10, 10; Stroke weight: 5 points; Dash: 0.1, Gap: 4; Cap: Butt; Join: Miter. Offset slightly by using the arrow keys.

MUMPS

45

Spurs

Studs

Type: Hobo, 100 points, Tracking +90.

First Stroke Settings: Fill: CMYK: 10, 45, 80, 10; Stroke Color: Black; Stroke weight: 6 points; Solid; Cap: Round; Join: Round.

Second Stroke Settings: Fill: none; Stroke Color: CMYK: 10, 13, 80, 10; Stroke weight: 3 points; Solid; Cap: Round; Join: Round.

Third Stroke Settings: Fill: none; Stroke Color: Black; Stroke weight: 2 points; Dash: 0.1; Gap: 8; Cap: Round; Join: Round.

Colors

Type: Hobo, 100 points, Tracking +90.

First Stroke Settings: Fill: None; Stroke Color: CMYK: 50, 10, 85, 10; Stroke weight: 8 points; Dash: 0.1; Gap: 10; Cap: Round; Join: Round.

Second Stroke Settings: Fill: None; Stroke Color: CMYK: 8, 80, 70, 8; Stroke weight: 8 points; Dash: 0.1; Gap: 20.1; Cap: Round; Join: Round.

Third Stroke Settings: Fill: None; Stroke Color: CMYK: 8, 80, 70, 8; Stroke weight: 3 points; Dash: 0.1; Gap: 10; Cap: Round; Join: Round.

Fourth Stroke Settings: Fill: None; Stroke Color: CMYK: 50, 10, 85, 10; Stroke weight: 3 points; Dash: 0.1; Gap: 20.1; Cap: Round; Join: Round.

More Colors

Type: Hobo, 100 points, Tracking +100.

First Stroke Settings: Fill: None; Stroke Color: CMYK: 100, 0, 100, 0; Stroke weight: 8 points; Solid; Cap: Butt; Join: Miter.

Second Stroke Settings: Fill: None; Stroke Color: CMYK: 0, 100, 100, 0; Stroke weight: 5 points; Solid; Cap: Butt; Join: Miter.

Third Stroke Settings: Fill: None; Stroke Color: Black; Stroke weight: 5 points; Dash: 8, Gap: 8; Cap: Butt; Join: Miter.

Rattler

The Ink Pen filter uses "hatches" to create textures. A hatch can be any object, but is usually something simple that the Ink Pen filter will duplicate many times and arrange according your directions. By creating a hatch made of type converted to outlines, you can use this filter to create a background of scattered type.

I Use the Type tool to enter the text. Because this effect is more about the arrangement of the type than the individual characteristics of the type, I like the effect better with a simple typeface that reads well, like AGaramond Bold. There also is no reason to use large type, so keep the point size low (12 points). Don't be concerned with the order you type the letters—the Ink Pen filter will randomly scatter them. However, because the Ink Pen filter cannot keep compound paths together, either use only letters that are not constructed from compound paths (letters that have no holes), like those shown here, or see the Variations to learn how to include all letters. Choose Type➡ Create Outlines. Leave the fill (black) and stroke (none) colors at the defaults.

2 Keep the type outlines selected and choose Filter➡Ink Pen➡ Hatches. Click the New button, and name the new hatch (Type Hatch).

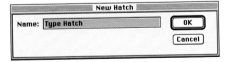

3 After clicking OK, the Hatch Dialog box will show a preview of the hatch in an arrangement. Notice that the letters have not stayed together. They have each been randomly dispersed. Click OK to create the hatch. You won't need the letters anymore, so delete them.

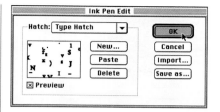

4 Use the Rectangle tool to create a box to contain the exploded type. Set the fill color of the rectangle with a color that can be used as the fill color for the type.

5 Choose Filter➡Ink Pen➡Effects. A large dialog box opens. Match the settings for Color, Background, and Fade to those shown in this figure. From the Hatch pop-up menu, choose the hatch you created in Step 2.

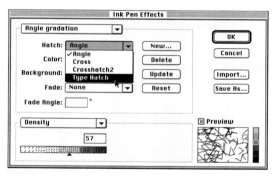

6 Beside the Preview window is a strip that contains six gray swatches. Select the third swatch from the bottom. These swatches provide one way to control the density of the dispersing type.

49

Dispersed

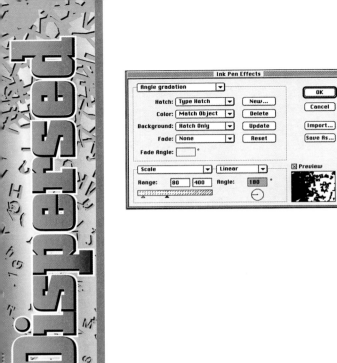

7 The pop-up menu in the bottom left corner of the dialog box contains the titles of five different settings. Select each title to change its settings. Set the Density to 57. For the Dispersion setting choose Constant from the right pop-up menu and set the Range to 145. Ignore the Thickness option that concerns stroke weights. For the Rotation setting, choose Random from the right pop-up menu, and set the Range values to −180, and 180. For the Scale setting, select Linear from the right pop-up menu, and set the Range values to 80 and 400. The last setting is the Scale Angle, and it must be coordinated with the Fade Angle above. The Scale Angle will determine from which side of the rectangle the dispersion begins. Try different angles and watch the change in the preview window.

Click OK to apply the effect.

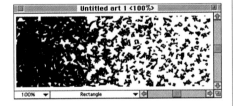

TIP The Fade option is also very useful. It enables you to fade the text to white or black, or along the current gradient. The Fade Angle determines the direction of the fade.

8 The type has been dispersed and the rectangle created in Step 4 now functions as a mask for the falling type. After applying the effect, the only objects selected are the letters, which are grouped. This is the perfect time to change the fill and stroke colors if you desire. I selected the Black, White gradient from the Swatches palette for the fill, and set the stroke color to black (Stroke weight: 0.5 point). Finally, I added a shadow.

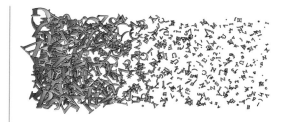

VARIATIONS

To use letters that are made of compound paths, you must turn them into paths that contain only one path. This task is easily accomplished with the Knife tool. After converting the type to outlines, select the Knife tool and a single letter that contains a hole. Click the Knife tool and then drag it from inside of the hole to outside of the hole, right across the letter. Congratulations, you've turned the compound path into a single path. Repeat this operation for each letter you want to include in the dispersed type. This trick comes with one limitation: you cannot include a stroke on this path, because the stroke will run across the letter at the point where the Knife tool cut across it.

51

Gradients

A gradient fill can be also be transferred to the letters. In Step 2, fill
the rectangle with a gradient and
use the Gradient tool to direct it.
Finish the rest of the steps with the
same settings.

Fill any Shape

Any path can be filled with the Ink
Pen filter. If the density of the type
is high enough, then the shape will
fill out well. Use the gray swatches
beside the Preview in the Ink Pen
dialog box to increase the
density. ■

FISH
TALES

The filters in the Filter➤Distort submenu can create some quick type transformations. The Punk & Bloat filter is especially useful for distorting the edges of the type. It works by twisting the control handles that direct the paths around the outlines of the type.

1 Use the Type tool to enter the text. This font is Arrus Bold at 95 points. Choose Type➤Create Outlines.

2 Choose Object➤Path➤Add Anchor Points. This command places one anchor point between every pair of anchor points on the path—nearly doubling the number of points. Each point will become a spike on the outline. If you want more spikes on your type, then you can reapply this command as many times as you want. Once is enough for this type.

3 Choose Filter➤Distort➤Punk & Bloat. Slide the marker toward the Punk side—until the percentage is around −9.

54

I used the type as a mask (see "Masked," page 104), and then gave the type an outline.

VARIATIONS

Here's what you get if you move the marker toward the Bloat side (8%); (Jacoby Black, 100 points).

Complete Step 1 (Boton Bold, 110 points, Tracking: 120).

Then choose Object➞Path➞Add Anchor Points. Repeat this step two more times. Choose Filter➞Distort➞Roughen (Size: 3%, Detail 10/in, Points: Corner). Then choose Filter➞Distort➞Punk & Bloat (Bloat 20%). Set the stroke settings as seen in this figure. Set the fill color to none.

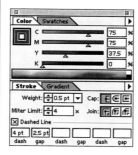

Here's the result:

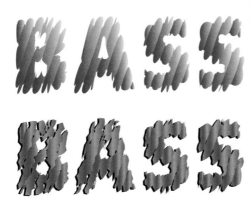

Punk (–20%) instead of Bloat in the last variation. See "Outlines" (page 114) for help creating multiple outlines.

Or ZigZag (Amount: 2, Ridges: 3/in, Smooth) instead of Bloat. Add a 1-point black stroke. Turn on the Dashed Line option (Dash: 0.1, Gap: 4). Set the Cap to Round.

Go to "Stripes" (page 232) and complete Steps 1 through 9 to create this striped type (Frutiger UltraBlack, 115 points, Tracking: 125, Horizontal Scale: 70%).

Select all and choose Filter➡ Distort➡Punk & Bloat. Set the marker to 24% (Bloat).

Fill the distorted stripes with a gradient. I used the Yellow, Red, Purple preset gradient.

One step more will produce this effect. Choose Filter➡Distort➡ Roughen (Size: 3%, Detail: 15/in, Corner). Add a 1-point black stroke, a custom gradient fill, and a solid black offset shadow.

56

Same effect, but I set the marker in the Punk & Bloat dialog box to −30% (Punk). ■

To create three-dimensional effects in Illustrator, you essentially have to build them yourself. That is, unless you have a third-party plug-in to do the work for you. Otherwise, use the methods in this technique to create relatively quick three-dimensional effects.

1 Use the Type tool to enter the text. Anything will work. I used Mistral at 90 points (Tracking: 25). Choose Type➡Create Outlines and press (Command-G)[Control-G] to group the letters. Color will not matter for now.

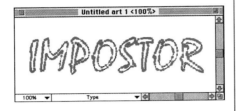

2 Optional step: Choose Object➡ Transform➡Transform Each, and set the Rotate angle to rotate each letter backwards just a bit (15°). This rotation will add a little tilt to the letters.

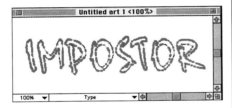

3 With the type still selected, double-click the Selection tool. A dialog box will appear. I want the sides of the type to fall to the left and down, so I want to raise the copies to the right and up. This means that I had to use a positive value for both the Horizontal and Vertical distances. I used .5-point for each. Press Copy. It will appear as if the left and bottom edges of the type have thickened slightly, very slightly—only .5-point.

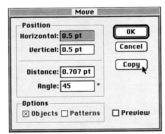

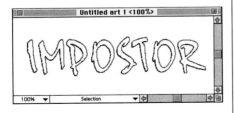

4 Press (Command-D)[Control-D] (Repeat Transform) as many times as it takes to build up the thickness of the letters. If you see gaps between the copies of type then undo the operation and decrease the Move distances used in Step 3. I pressed (Command-D)[Control-D] 12 times.

5 The top copy should still be selected. Set the fill color (CMYK 0, 50, 100, 0,) and set the stroke color to black for the type. The color of the receding sides is easily changed by selecting all copies of the type, except the top one, and setting colors. I made the sides CMYK: 75, 95, 5, 5.

Fattened 3D

1 Use the Type tool to enter the text (Mistral, 100 points). Choose Type➡Create Outlines. Set the fill color to CMYK: 50, 100, 100, 0, and set the stroke color to white.

2 Copy the type and press (Command-B)[Control-B] to paste a copy in back. Set the stroke weight to 3 points and set the stroke color (CMYK 100, 100, 0, 0).

3 Paste another copy in back. Set the stroke color to the color for the fattened part of the letters (25% Black). Raising the stroke weight will create the thickness of the type. I set the stroke weight at 8 points for this 100-point type.

4 Use the arrow keys to move the thick type—just a little—down and to the right. I pressed each key about four times.

TIP Make sure that you don't move the type too far or you will see gaps between the type and the fat shadow as shown here.

5 Copy the type and paste a copy in back (Command-B)[Control-B]. Raise the stroke weight a couple of points to 10, and set the stroke color. I used the same stroke color as in Step 2.

Boxed Type

1 Enter the text using the Type tool. I used Impact at 80 points. Set the stroke color and set the fill color. Choose Type➡Create Outlines.

2 Optional Step: Double-click the Shear tool and set the angle at −20° (Horizontal). Double-click the Rotate tool to rotate the type outlines (10°). These transformations will make the letters appear as if they are receding.

3 Hold down the Shift and (Option)[Alt] keys while dragging the type outlines to create a copy directly above the original.

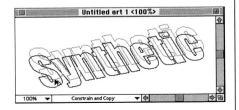

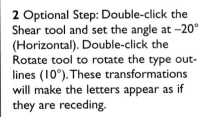

4 Choose File➡Preferences➡ General and make sure that the Snap to Point option is turned on.

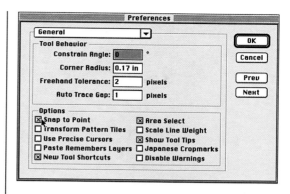

5 Now the tough part. Select the Pen tool. The two copies of type will serve as guides for drawing the sides. See the shape I drew here.

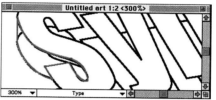

6 These shapes will create the sides. As you complete each shape cut it, then select the top copy of the type and press (Command-B) [Control-B] to paste the new boxes in back. Use the same method to make sure that all of the correct pieces are on top of each other. You can also set their fill color as you create each.

TIP The Send Backward, Send Forward commands move the object one level forward or backward. Use these commands to help organize the new side planes. **Send Backward: (Command-[)[Control-[ ]. Send Forward: (Command-]) [Control-]].**

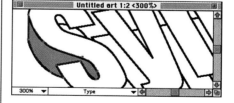

61

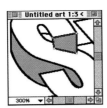 

7 Here's a trick: If you know that part of the shape will be covered by another shape, then don't worry about what that part of the shape looks like. Draw the visible part to match, then close the path and send it behind the other shape.

Some shapes may repeat, like the shapes that cap the bottoms of the "n." After drawing the first shape, you can make a copy to use for the second shape.

8 As you create the shapes color each appropriately. Make sure that all pieces on the same side of the type are the same color.

VARIATIONS

Use a similar technique to create this box frame type. Instead of drawing shapes, use the Pen tool to draw only the lines that connect the two copies of the type (make sure that the fill color is none). This is much easier than drawing the shapes. However, you will have to draw a few extra lines that would have been hidden if the type was filled.

Select all and copy. Fill the top and bottom copies of the type with two different colors. Choose Object➡ Pathfinder➡Soft (50%). Press (Command-F)[Control-F] to paste a copy in front. Then set the fill color of the pasted objects to none.

KPT Vector Effects 3D Transform

It's tough to beat third-party filters and software when it comes to creating three-dimensional type effects. Change the type to outlines and choose Filter➡KPT Vector Effects➡3D Transform. ■

After you have used some of the third party filters available for Illustrator, you will wonder how Adobe could have not included these filters as resident features. Throughout the techniques in this book, some of these filters have been used to create variations on the described effects. Following are more things you can do with these filters. Check out the demo versions of these filters included on the *Illustrator Type Magic* CD-ROM. See Appendix B, "What's on the CD-ROM," for information on accessing the demos.

KPT Vector Effects

Thirteen filters reside in the KPT Vector Effects submenu, including some very useful filters for one-step type treatments. Vector Effects is certainly the most useful set of filters for creating one-step type effects. Also, the Inset filter, which performs the same function as Illustrator's Offset Path feature, is a welcome substitute if you can put up with bouncing into the dark and overbearing world of the KPT interface. Here are a few type treatments created by the Vector Effects.

KPT 3D Transform

Everyone needs to create three-dimensional type sometimes. For many 3D type effects, this all-purpose tool will eliminate the need for a second application such as Adobe Dimensions.

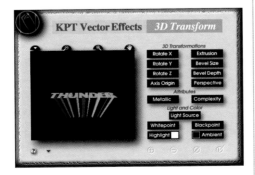

KPT Neon

This filter uses the fill color of the selected object as the base color for the neon effect. The interior of the letters will become a lighter variation of this color. There are only two settings in this filter: Brightness is self-explanatory; the Amount value determines how far the neon spreads out from the selected path.

65

KPT Warp Frame

This filter allows you to pinch, stretch, and squeeze type by choosing one of the dozens of presets or by manually manipulating individual points.

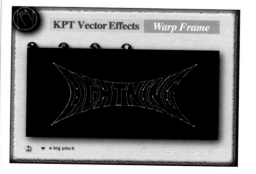

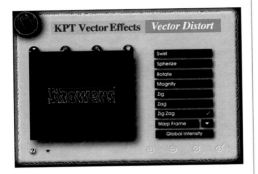

KPT Vector Distort

There are seven standard distortion effects in this filter: Swirl, Spherize, Rotate, Magnify, Zig, Zag, and ZigZag (shown here). More than one effect can be applied at the same time, by creating new "Influences" (Command-N) [Control-N].

KPT Sketch

This is another two-setting filter that separates and distorts stroke and fill colors in order to create a sketchy look.

KPT Shadowland

Useful for creating quick drop shadows, this filter can blend a shadow from any color to any color.

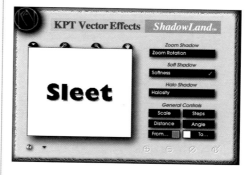

Extensis VectorTools

Another large set of plug-ins for Illustrator, the VectorTools palettes can be accessed through the VectorTools menu, which appears in the menu bar after installing the software. Particularly useful for creating type effects is the VectorShape palette. Also, the VectorColor palette is used throughout this book to create random color effects.

VectorShape

The VectorShape palette allows you to wrap type onto four different types of preset objects: spheres, cylinders, cones (shown here), and stars. The shape of each of these object types is editable from the palette.

VectorColor

The VectorColor palette is used throughout this book mostly for its Randomize color feature, which applies random colors to all selected objects. Other useful features include: Brightness/Contrast adjustment, Grayscale converter, and Multitone converter for creating duotones.

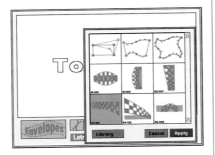

Letraset Envelopes

Shaping type never had so many options. Select the type to be transformed and choose Filter➡ Letraset➡Envelopes to open the Envelopes dialog box. The full version of this filter contains many envelopes, each a unique transformation. It works much like the KPT Warp Frame filter.

Infinite FX

This plug-in from BeInfinite contains 55 preset effects for distorting type. Choose an effect, and then use the controls on the interface to alter it.

Stylist

AlienSkin's Stylist plug-in uses a floating palette as its interface. Stylist enables you to create styles that can be saved, and then applied to numerous objects. This feature would be great if you had to create 20 different words in the same effect. ▧

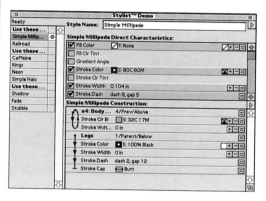

In this technique, a palette of strokes that blend from the glow color to the background color is created. Then the attributes (color and weight) of the strokes in the palette are transferred one at a time to layered copies of the type outlines. Don't let the fractions scare you. The numbers don't need to be precise—approximate guesses will work. Keep in mind that the number of steps used in the Blend dialog box determines the smoothness of the glow. The weight and change in color of the strokes determines how rapidly the glow colors blend.

1 Use the Type tool to enter the text. I used Anna at 130 points. Choose Type➤Create Outlines. Set the fill color for the type, and set the stroke color to none.

2 Use the Pen tool to draw a short vertical line away from the type. Set the stroke color to the color for the highlight of the glow, set the fill color to none, and set the stroke weight to 1 point.

3 Grab the line with the Selection tool and hold down the Shift and (Option)[Alt] keys as you drag the line to the right, about this far, to make a copy. Set the stroke weight to three times the spread of the glow. I chose 20 points, which will create a glow that extends approximately 7 points from the edge of the type. Set the stroke color to the color of the background (CMYK: 0, 0, 0, 0).

4 Select both lines, then get the Blend tool and click once on the top of the first line. Click a second time (after the dash appears below the crosshairs) on the top of the second line.

5 A dialog box opens asking for the number of steps to include in the blend. The more steps you include the smoother the blend will be, but the more work you will have to do in Step 12. I set the number to 20. If you match the number of Steps to the stroke weight chosen for the line created in Step 3, then you should be okay.

Click OK and a series of lines are filled in between the two originals. This is the beginning of the palette. In order to produce a smoother glow, the palette will need to be adjusted. Press (Command-Shift-G) [Control-Shift-G] to ungroup the lines.

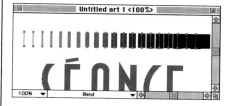

6 Select and delete the middle third of the palette of lines. Then select the first line after the gap. Set the stroke weight of this line to half of the stroke weight used in Step 3—10 points.

7 Select the two middle lines that are separated by the gap. Get the Blend tool and use it again as in Steps 4 and 5. Set the number of Steps to 1/4 the number of steps used in Step 5—5 steps. Press (Command-Shift-G)[Control-Shift-G] to ungroup the lines.

8 Then delete all of the lines between the 10-point stroke used previously and the thickest line. Select the last two lines.

9 Use the Blend tool again to create a final blend between these two lines. The number of Steps should be equal to 1/3 the number of Steps used in Step 5—7 steps. The palette is now ready for applying to the type. Arrange the type and palette so that both can be seen in the image window.

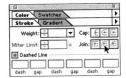

10 Select all of the lines, find the Stroke palette, and click the Round button for the Joins. This will give the glow rounded corners.

TIP After you have created this palette of lines, save the Illustrator document to save the palette. You can open it later and follow the remaining steps to add the same glow to any type.

11 Select the type paths, copy them, and hide them (Command-U) [Control-U]. Paste a copy of the type in back (Command-B) [Control-B]. Get the Eyedropper tool and double-click the thinnest line. The stroke and fill colors of the line, as well as the stroke weight, are transferred to the type path.

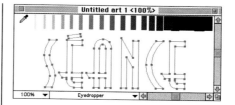

12 Press (Command-B)[Control-B] to paste another copy of the type in back. Use the Eyedropper tool as in Step 11 to double-click on the next thinnest line. Repeat this step until all of the lines in the palette have been used. The glow will grow gradually as you proceed.

13 Press (Command-Shift-U) [Control-Shift-U] to reveal the original type. Setting the stroke color to the glow highlight color intensifies the glow (stroke weight: 2 points). Set the fill color for the type to the Steel Bar gradient.

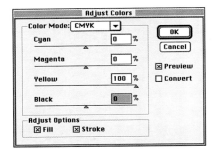

VARIATIONS

Ghosted

Set the fill color of the original type to the same color as the background.

Color

To change the color of the glow, simply select all of the glow strokes and choose Filter➡Colors➡Adjust. Use the sliders to find a new color.

Rounded and Glowing Effects

This example shows a glow behind type created by the similar "Rounded" effect on page 172. ∎

Filling type with a gradient is perhaps the quickest and easiest way to transform dull type into something that jumps off the page (or screen, as the case may be these days). The following is a smattering of basic gradient effects to get you started, and to help you create the numerous other effects in this book that use gradients as a key ingredient.

The Gradient Tool

1 Use the Type tool to enter the text. I used Freehand 471 at 150 points. To fill type with a gradient you must convert the type into outline paths. Choose Type➡ Create Outlines.

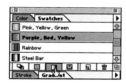

2 While the type is still selected, find the Swatches palette and click the gradient button at the bottom of the palette. Then click on one of the gradients in the list to select it.

3 I chose the Purple, Red, Yellow gradient for this type.

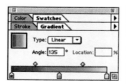

4 Each letter is filled with the gradient. You can change the direction of the gradient in each of the letters by changing the angle on the Gradient palette. I set the angle to 135° for this example.

5 If you want the gradient to flow through all of the letters selected, then select the Gradient tool, click, and drag it across the type in the direction you want the gradient to flow.

TIP If you have run the gradient across all of the letters and decide that you want it to extend through each letter separately, then select all of the letters and set the gradient angle on the Gradient palette. The gradient will automatically revert to filling each letter separately.

6 If you want to change the direction of the gradient within each of the letters, then select each letter one at a time, and use the Gradient tool on each as described in Step 5. Or set the Angle on the Gradient palette.

77

VARIATIONS

The effect employed for this type relies on manipulation of the direction of the gradient. The type was cut into stripes (see page 232), and then all stripes were filled with a gradient. Every other stripe was selected and the direction was changed from 0° to 180°. You can see the difference in effect between a three-color gradient (in "Ten") and a two-color gradient (in "Nine"); "Eight" is filled with the Steel bar gradient.

Creating Gradients

1 To create your own gradient you must use an existing gradient as a template. Find the Gradient palette (Window➡Show Gradient), and either click the Gradient preview on the Gradient palette or choose an existing gradient from the Swatches palette. You will save some time if you choose a gradient that is similar to the gradient you want to create.

2 To change the colors in the gradient, click one of the markers below the gradient preview (the triangle at the top of the marker will turn black when selected). Use the Color palette to choose a color for the marker. I changed this yellow to a blue (CMYK: 50, 5, 10, 0).

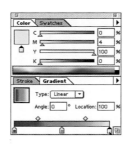

3 To add colors to the gradient, click the pointer below the gradient preview, and a new marker will appear. The color in the gradient at which the new stop was inserted will be assigned as the color of the new stop. Choose its color as described in Step 2 (CMYK: 50, 5, 50, 0).

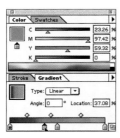

4 To remove a color from the gradient, click on the color stop with the pointer and drag it off of the palette.

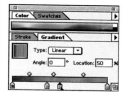

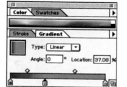

5 The diamond markers above the gradient preview change the midpoint of the gradation between two colors. Here I shifted a diamond marker to make the grading from the dark blue to the green more abrupt.

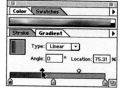

TIP	The location of the color stops and diamond markers can also be set numerically. Select a marker and type in a percentage in the Location box.

6 To save a gradient, click the Gradient preview icon and drag it to the Swatches palette. A new swatch named New Gradient will show up in the Swatches list. To rename the new swatch, double-click on it in the Swatches palette.

7 Here is the gradient applied to type. Use the Gradient tool to direct the gradient as described earlier in the "Gradient Tool" section.

Striped Gradients

A gradient with many colors in it will produce a striped effect. You can also use the gradient palette to create a striped effect that contains no color grading. To create an abrupt color change, place two color stops directly on top of each other. In this gradient there is a stop placed at Location 25%. Click to the right of that color stop to create a new marker.

Use the Color or Swatches palette to select a new color for the stop (CMYK: 0, 0, 0, 0). Then change the Location for that stop to same Location used earlier: 25%.

You can repeat these steps to produce a multicolored striped gradient.

Rounded Effect

The gradient shown here was created to produce a rounded effect when applied to type.

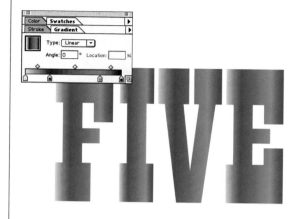

Radial Gradients

There are two types of gradients: Radial and Linear. This setting is on the Gradient palette.

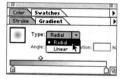

Each letter here was filled with a simple two-color radial gradient.

A Radial Gradient Pattern

Create a circle and fill it with a radial blend. Then duplicate the circle and arrange the duplicates so the edge colors overlap.

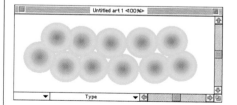

81

Place the type outlines on top of the radial gradients. While the type only is selected, choose Object➡Compound Paths➡Make to turn the type into a single compound path. Select all, and choose Object➡Masks➡Make.

Type Cut From Gradients

Create a radial blur with a gradient that fades to the background color, place a letter on top, and convert the letter to outlines. Select the blur and the letter, and choose Object➡Pathfinder➡Minus Front. I did this for each of these letters.

Use the same radial blur. Place the type outlines on top. Set the stroke weight to 4 points, and choose Objects➡Path➡Outline Path. Set the stroke weight to 1 point, and set the fill color to the same radial gradient used for the background. Use the Gradient tool on each letter separately (see Step 5 on page 77) to drag the gradient from the bottom of the type to the top.

Crumbled Gradients

A gradient fill adds an extra touch to any effect. This type was broken up using the "Crumbling" technique (page 34), then filled with a gradient. ■

You could spend days running through the possibilities issued by the Ink Pen filter, which masks multiples of shapes called "hatches" into objects such as type outlines. The direct application of this filter can create some great effects. The following steps show you how to work with the filter to get even more out of it. Once you understand the filter, you can begin to create your own hatches. Be careful when using this filter because it can produce memory-intensive and time-consuming graphics that will bog down performance.

1 Use the Type tool to enter the text (Present at 110 points). This is a fill effect that is most visible inside thick display typefaces. Choose Type➡Create Outlines, Object➡Compound Paths➡Make, and copy the type.

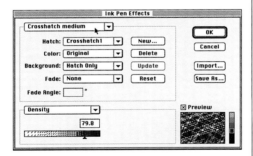

2 Choose Filter➡Ink Pen➡Effects. What a dialog box! From the pop-up menu, choose the Crosshatch medium preset hatching effect.

Check out the effect in the Preview window at the bottom-right of the dialog box and click OK.

3 The crosshatching is a nice effect in itself, but there is more you can do. The type now acts as a mask for lines created by the Ink Pen filter. Press (Command-A)[Control-A] to reselect the type with the new lines. Change the fill color for all of the selected objects from none to black to set up the Crop pathfinder (which will not work unless the objects have fill colors). This is just a way to trick it into working on the type.

4 Choose Object➡Pathfinder➡ Crop to get rid of lines outside of the type. This operation may take a minute or two, but it will save time later when you apply colors, save, and/or print the file. In this close-up you can see that the lines now end at the borders of the type outlines, which, by the way, have been deleted by the Crop pathfinder.

5 Set the stroke weight to 1 point, then choose Object➡Path➡ Outline Path to change the strokes to fills. The only onscreen change will be a slight thickening of the lines.

6 Set the fill color for the lines with a gradient (Purple, Red, Yellow). This is the advantage of converting the lines to fills—you can use a gradient fill.

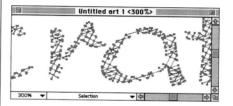

85

TIP One way to reduce the processing time for this effect is to reduce the Density setting in the Ink Pen dialog box. Choose Density from the pop-up menu at the bottom of the dialog box, and use the sliding marker to reduce the density. You might need to set the point size in Step 5 a little higher to fill out the type outlines. Of course, this will also affect the look of the effect, producing thicker hatches.

VARIATIONS

The Ink Pen filter uses, if you choose, the fill color from the type to color the hatches in the effect. Gradients are an especially crowd-pleasing fill color for this filter. Fill the type with a gradient. Then copy the type.

Choose Filter➡Ink Pen➡Effects and select the Fiberglass medium preset from the pop-up menu. Then choose Match Object from the Color pop-up menu...

...to get this result.

Paste a copy of the type in back (Command-B)[Control-B]. Fill the type with a new gradient (Rainbow) and use the Gradient tool to direct the gradient if desired. I also added strokes.

Creating Hatches

There are two menu items in the Ink Pen sub menu: Effects and Hatches. The Effects item is for applying the filter to artwork as in the above steps. The Hatches item enables you to create and edit your own hatches to use in the Effects item. Follow these steps to create and use a custom hatch.

1 Create an object to use as a hatch. Don't create a complex graphic for the hatch. The more complicated the hatch, the longer it will to take to process, render, and print an applied effect. Keep the shape simple and use the Ink Effects dialog box options to create the desired look. Also create the object near the size that it will be in the type. For this example, I created a simple hexagon that is about 15 points across (fill: black, stroke: none).

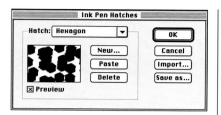

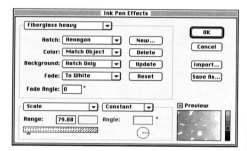

2 While the object is selected, choose Filter➡Ink Pen➡Hatches. The Ink Pen dialog box opens. Click the new button, and name the new hatch (Hexagon). The preview window will show the new hatch arranged in a random pattern. Click OK to create the new hatch.

3 Use the Type tool to enter the text (Frutiger Black, 110 points). Choose Type➡Create Outlines. I set a different fill color for each letter.

4 Choose Filter➡Ink Pen➡Effects. You can now choose the hatch (Hexagon) just created in the Hatches pop-up menu. Fiddle with the settings and watch the limited, but helpful, preview in the bottom-right corner. I first chose the Fiberglass heavy preset, then set the Hatch to Hexagon, the Fade To White, the Color to Match Object, and the Scale to approximately 79.

Click OK to apply the effect. ∎

Divide the type into pieces and then reunite them using the Pathfinders. The gradients added in the Variations greatly improve this effect.

1 Use the Type tool to enter the letters to interlock. I used Korinna at 150 points. Choose Type➡ Create Outlines.

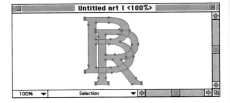

2 Position the letters over each other in an arrangement that allows parts of the two letters to overlap. I chose two letters that I knew would weave together well.

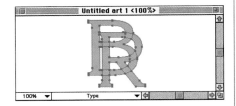

3 Select both letters and choose Object➡Pathfinder➡Divide, then press (Command-Shift-G)[Control-Shift-G] to ungroup them. The type has been separated into all of the shapes created by their overlapping lines. You won't see much change on screen, except for a few new points added.

4 You now need to determine which parts of the letters will run over the top and which parts will run underneath the other letter(s). Pick one of the letters and select all of its parts that will not be underneath any of the other letters. See my selections here.

5 Choose Object➡Pathfinder➡ Unite to join these parts as one shape. You will see the dividing lines disappear. Set the fill and stroke colors for the type. You can already see the interlocking effect.

6 Pick another letter and again select the parts that will not run underneath any of the other letters. Then choose Object➡ Pathfinder➡Unite. Set the fill and stroke colors for this letter. Repeat this procedure for all letters.

With Shadows

1 Adding a few shadows is a great complement to this effect. You will need to divide the letters so that there are small shapes near the overlapped parts of the letters. Complete the previous steps, then select the Knife tool. Drag it across one of the letters just before it dips under another letter. You can see the cuts I made here. These new parts will contain the shadows.

2 Deselect all objects (Command-Shift-A)[Control-Shift-A]. Activate the Swatches palette and click on the Black, White gradient. Activate the Gradient palette, which now displays the Black, White gradient. Select all of the new small pieces for that letter.

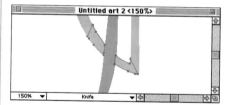

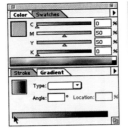

3 Activate the Color palette. The color proxy (preview swatch) will show the fill color for these parts. Click the color and then drag it from the color proxy to the left edge of the Black, White gradient on the Gradient palette. After dragging the color, there should be only one tag below the left side of the gradient. If the white tag is still there, press (Command-Z) [Control-Z] and try it again. The selected pieces of the type will fill with the gradient.

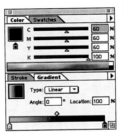

4 Click the black icon (on the right) below the gradient. Go to the Color palette and select CMYK from the arrow pop-up menu. Then set the C, M, and Y percentages to 60 (leave the K percentage at 100). This richer black will improve the gradient.

5 To save the gradient, activate the Swatches palette, and drag the proxy (Preview icon) on the Gradient palette to the Swatches palette. The swatch will automatically be named New Gradient Swatch. If you want to rename the palette, double-click the new gradient to open the Swatch Options dialog box, in which you can enter a new name.

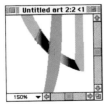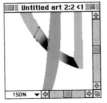

6 Press (Command-Shift-A) [Control-Shift-A] to deselect all objects. Then select the Gradient tool and only one of the small type pieces, which is now filled with the new gradient. Drag the Gradient tool along the type piece toward the area in which it dips under another letter.

7 Use the Gradient tool to redirect the gradient in all pieces of this letter.

8 Create new gradients for each letter, and direct them with the Gradient tool.

Strokes, shadows, and boxes. ▪

Use the Transform Each feature to mix up the type. This feature is especially useful when you want to add a little variation to a lot of type.

1 Use the Type tool to enter the text. I used Gadzoox at 100 points. Choose Type➡Create Outlines.

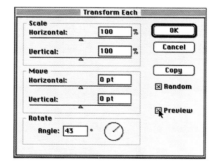

2 Choose Object➡Transform➡ Transform Each. A fun dialog box opens. To jumble each letter of the type differently, turn on the Random and Preview options. Then set the Rotate Angle to about 26°. The letters will Rotate to varying degrees.

3 Watch the preview. If you don't like the particular random arrangement, simply click off the Preview option and then click it on again. For more jumble, raise the Rotate Angle.

Find something you like, click OK, and you're done.

TOOLBOX

Extensis
VectorTools

4 The extra-thick look of this type was created by using the Fattened variation of the "Fake 3D" effect on page 58.

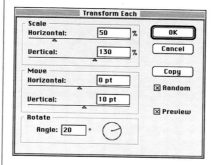

VARIATIONS

For something a little more drastic, play with the other settings. Here are the settings I used…

…and here is the type (Schadow, 65 points).

For some overlapping, jumbled type, set the Horizontal Scale setting at 200% and the Rotate angle to 15°. Keep the Random option turned on. (This type was already placed on an undulating path—see "On Paths," page 128.)

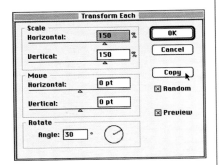

Jumbled Copies

If you click the Copy button in the Transform Each box instead of OK, then you can layer the jumbled type. Here are the settings I used:

Select all the letters and choose Object➤Pathfinder➤Divide.

Finally, from VectorTools VectorColor palette I clicked the Randomize button. (Turn off the Match Color option on the arrow pop-out menu.) If you have KPT Vector Effects, then you could use the Randomize feature in the KPT ColorTweak filter instead of the VectorColor palette.

I used the same method (and settings) for this variation. Copy the type before applying the Transform Each filter. Do not click the Copy button in the Transform Each dialog box (just click OK). Press (Command-F)[Control-F] to paste a new copy of the type in front of the rotated original. Use the Transform Each feature again to rotate this new copy of the type. Keep pasting and transforming as much as you want. This type consists of seven copies of the original type. Again I used the VectorColor Randomize feature. Then pasted and transformed a final copy in which I set the fill color to none and set the stroke color to black. ■

98

The Pathfinder commands are great at cutting objects, including type outlines. Cutting out type is as simple as stacking type on top of an object and using the Pathfinders to cut the type outlines from the underlying object. Here are a few methods that use various Pathfinders to knock type out from other elements.

1 Use the Shape or Create tools to create a shape to cut the text from. A simple circle will do, but so will a complicated illustration. I used the Star tool to create this shape. If you have several shapes, select them and choose Object➡Compound Paths➡Make to join them into a compound path.

2 I used the Type tool to enter this 96-point Helvetica ExtraCompressed text (Tracking: 80). Choose Type➡ Create Outlines. Position the type on top of the background.

3 Select the background shape and the type outline. Choose Object➡ Pathfinder➡Minus Front. A single compound path that defines the shape with the type cut out of it remains.

4 The new shape that includes the cutout type will be selected. I added a shadow to complete the effect. Copy the selection, paste it in back (Command-B)[Control-B], and set the fill color to black (or another color) for the shadow. Then use the arrow keys to nudge it away from the original type.

VARIATIONS

Type in Type

Use the same technique to knock out type from type.

Frogs jump and

Twirling Knockouts

After changing the original type to outlines, I placed a copy of the type directly on top of the original type and used the Twirl tool to slightly twist the copied type only. I then selected both copies and chose Object➡Pathfinder➡Exclude.

I set the fill color of the type to white and placed an object behind it. It looks like the white is cut out of the background, but in fact the white is the type's fill color and the interiors of the letters are cut out to reveal the placed object behind.

99

Holes

After converting the type to outlines, copy it. Place objects over the type, like my circular "bullet holes."

Select the type and the objects. Choose Object➤Pathfinder➤ Exclude.

In order to place a little more emphasis on the type outlines, add a stroke to the type. To do this, press (Command-F)[Control-F] to place a copy of the original type in front, then set the fill color to none, set the stroke color to anything you like (CMYK 0, 100, 50, 0), and set the stroke weight to 1 point.

Half and Half

Some Photoshop filters can be copied directly from Photoshop's Plug-ins folder (Adobe Photoshop➤ Plug-ins) into Illustrator's Plug-ins folder (Adobe Illustrator 7.0➤ Plug-ins) and then used from within Illustrator. I copied the Spherize filter into Illustrator's Plug-ins folder. Remember, you must copy the plug-in before launching Illustrator. After launching Illustrator, place some type partially over a background of the same color.

Select the type and the background, and choose Object➤Pathfinder➤ Exclude.

Place a colored background behind everything. Select all of the objects and choose Object➤Pathfinder➤ Divide. Press (Command-Shift-G) [Control-Shift-G] to ungroup the objects. Deselect all pieces that are outside of the circle.

Choose Object➤Rasterize. In the dialog box that opens, choose the Color Model and Resolution that suit your needs (I used RGB and 150 ppi). Once rasterized, the object is treated as a placed object—you cannot access individual parts that make up the object.

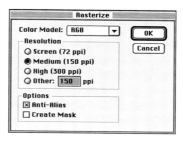

Press (Command-[)[Control-[ ] until the object moves behind all of the other (non-rasterized, non-spherized) objects. I had to press it 10 times.

Choose Filter➤Distort➤Spherize to access the filter copied from Photoshop previously. Set the amount at 75%.

TIP Remember, Photoshop filters will only work on rasterized objects. Also, there are two Distort submenus under the Filter menu. The Spherize filter is under the second Distort submenu (the first will be grayed out if you have a rasterized object selected). ■

Make an offset shadow, then use the Pathfinder commands to keep it inside the type outlines. Here are three different versions of this easy technique.

Quick

1 Use the Type tool to enter the text. This quick effect will work with any type. It is even easy to apply to other effects. I used Utopia SemiBold Italic at 120 points. Choose Type➡Create Outlines. Set the fill color for the type (I used the Polka Dot pattern fill), and set the stroke color to none.

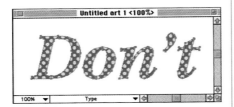

2 Group the letters (Command-G) [Control-G], Copy them, and then paste the copy in front (Command-F) [Control-F]. Set the fill color to none and set the stroke color to the color for the lip (CMYK: 36, 0, 80, 0). Then set the stroke weight to the width of the lip (3 points).

3 Copy the stroked type, then paste it in back (Command-B) [Control-B] so that it is placed between the filled type and the stroked type. Use the arrow keys to shift the shadow away from the lip. I pressed the Down and Left Arrow keys two times each. Set the stroke color for the shadow (CMYK: 30, 30, 30, 100).

Contained

After completing Steps 1 through 3, complete three more steps to contain the lip shadow within the type.

4 Choose Object➡Path➡Outline Path to convert the stroke into a filled compound path. In the figure you can see that the black stroke now has edges on the inside and outside. Choose Object➡ Compound Paths➡Make to combine all of the shadow paths into one compound path.

5 Deselect the shadow, and select the stroked type that is on top. Choose Object➡Compound Paths➡Make again to combine the stroked type paths into a single compound path. Copy the paths. Then Shift-select the compound shadow path to add it to the selected stroked type. Choose Object➡Pathfinder➡Crop. The parts of the shadow that fell outside the letter will be cut off, and the stroked type will disappear.

6 Paste the stroked type in front (Command-F)[Control-F].

VARIATIONS

Complete Steps 1 through 3, and then select the top copy of the type outlines, and set the stroke weight to 1 point. ■

Type outlines can be turned into masks, and then used for a variety of effects. You can think of a mask as allowing the type outlines to become a container, and it could conceivably contain anything. Here are instructions for creating basic masks for photographs and other art. Other effects that use type outlines as masks are: "Ink Pen," "Patterns," "Rasterized," and "Stripes."

The Basic Mask

1 Choose File➡Place. Find an image to import and click OK.

2 Use the Type tool to enter the text. A heavy font works best for masking photographs, but the effect will work anything. I used Anna at 45 points and Pepita at 120 points. The swoosh was made by copying, pasting, rotating, and scaling the bottom of the "B." Select all of the type and choose Type➡Create Outlines. Then choose Object➡Compound Paths➡Make.

3 Select the type and the photograph and choose Object➡Masks➡Make.

TOOLBOX

KPT Vector Effects

4 You cannot put a stroke on type outlines that are being used as a mask. If you want to put a stroke on the type, copy the type, select the mask and the placed image, and paste the type in back (Command-B) [Control-B]. Then set the stroke weight and set the stroke color. You will have to raise the stroke weight a little higher than normal because the stroke is coming out from behind the mask, rather than laying on top of it. I created a 4-point black stroke and shifted it down and to the left. I copied that stroke, pasted it in back, changed the stroke color to a green, and again, shifted it away from the type.

TIP **After creating a mask, you can still adjust the mask to reveal a different part of the image. Use the Selection tool to select either the placed image or the type outlines. Drag the selection to adjust the masked area.**

VARIATIONS

To create the illusion that the type has been pushed up from the photograph, after Step 1, make a copy of the placed image and paste it in front (Command-F)[Control-F] of the original copy. In Step 3, select the type and the placed image in front only. Add the black stroke mentioned in Step 4 (but not the green one). Select the stroke, the mask (the type outlines), and the front copy of the placed image.

Nudge them the same distance as you shifted the stroke in Step 4, but shift them in the opposite direction—up and to the right in this case.

Multiple Items

You can mask as many objects or images into type outlines as you want. To make this type, create random boxes behind the type and fill them with several of Illustrator's predefined patterns.

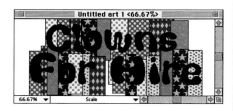

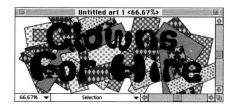

Select the boxes and choose Object➡Transform➡Transform Each (Rotate: 180, Random). You will most likely have to copy and paste a few of the filled boxes to cover gaps created by the Random rotating. Randomly rotating the filled boxes will take the rigidity out of the patchwork fills.

Convert the type into outlines. Select all of the type and choose Object➡Compound Path➡Make. Select all (the type outlines and the pattern fills) and choose Object➡Masks➡Make. A couple of outlines and a black background finished this image.

Cropped Masks

If you are masking paths (not photographs, or other imported artwork) and you are certain that you will not want to shift the image to show a different part of the background objects through the mask, then you can crop the artwork to get rid of everything that is not included inside the type outlines.

Make sure the type has been made into a single compound path (Step 1). Copy the type outlines (Freehand521, 110 points). By cropping, instead of masking, you get rid of the cumbersome hidden parts of the masked objects that always seem to get in the way when trying to edit other objects near the type. It will also reduce the file size.

Skip Step 3 and instead do the following. Select the type and all background items. Choose Object➡Pathfinder➡Crop.

After the Crop pathfinder has been applied, the type outlines disappear. To add a stroke or shadow, paste in the copy made in the first step.

Everywhere a Mask

The type was created with KPT VectorEffects 3D Transform. Use the top type outlines as a mask for a photo.

107

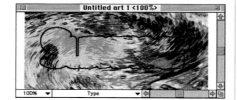

Bigger Masks

Squeeze the type together (as in "Overlapped," page 120). This is 100-point ITC Kabel Bold with a Tracking value of −100. Choose Type➡Create Outlines. Press (Command-G)[Control-G] to group the type.

Copy the type. Choose Object➡ Pathfinder➡Unite. Then Object➡ Path➡Offset Path. The offset value will determine how far the masked image projects beyond the type outlines. I set the offset to 6 points (Joins: Round). Choose Object➡ Pathfinder➡Unite again to get rid of the odd shapes created by off-setting the path. The type outlines that resulted from the first Unite remain. Delete them. Place the image behind the type.

Select the image and the united, off-set type (as seen in previous step). Choose Object➡Masks➡Make. Paste the type back in and add strokes to complete the effect.

Type in Type

Use the same methods to mask type into type. Convert all type to outlines and treat the type as the objects earlier in this technique (Futura ExtraBold and Freehand575). ▇

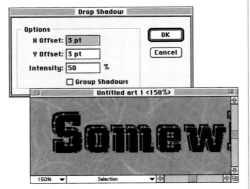

This technique creates an offset copy of the type that is separated from the type by a gap. It is similar to a drop shadow, but a little fancier because of the see-through space between the type and the shadow. In fact, the Drop Shadow filter is used in this technique to eliminate a step in setting the type up for the Minus Front pathfinder.

1 Use the Type tool to enter the text. This effect will work well with almost every font, but works best with fonts with squared features. I used City Bold at 75 points. Choose Type➡Create Outlines. I placed a background behind the type to show that the gap is truly transparent and not just the same color as the background.

2 Choose Filter➡Stylize➡Drop Shadow. The Drop Shadow filter will paste a copy of the type in back and move it at the same time, saving you a step. You can move the type in any direction. I set the X and Y offsets to 3 points. This offset distance will establish the gap between the type and offset. Ignore the Intensity percentage and turn off the Group Shadows option. Click OK and press (Command-8) [Control-8] to turn the shadows into a compound path.

TIP The Drop Shadow filter sends the shadow all the way to the back of the image. If the type is in front of a background, then the Drop Shadow filter will place the shadow behind the background. Immediately after applying the Drop Shadow filter, bring the shadow forward by pressing (Command-]) [Control-]] until the shadow shows up.

3 Press (Command-Shift-E) [Control-Shift-E] to reopen the Drop Shadow filter dialog box. Set the offset a little lower this time. These offset distances establish the weight of the offset type. I set them both at 1 point. Again, press (Command-8)[Control-8] to make the new shadow a compound path. There should now be three stacked copies of the type.

4 Select both copies of the type created by the Drop Shadow filter, but do not select the original type. Choose Object➡Pathfinder➡Minus Front.

5 Set the fill color for the offset type.

Set the fill color to none, set the stroke color to black, and set the stroke weight to 1 point for the offset type.

Simply delete the original type, and set the fill color and set the stroke color for the offset.

A Different Kind of Offset

Place two copies of the type on top of each other. Copy one of the copies. Set different fill colors for each. Select all of the type and choose Object➡Pathfinder➡Soft (50%). Paste the copied type in front (Command-F)[Control-F] . Set the fill color to none and set the stroke color to black (1 point). Shift the outline. ▪

From simple to complex, Illustrator is great at transforming type outlines. Most of the work is done by varying stroke weights and colors.

1 Enter the text using the Type tool. I used Brush Script at 110 points (Tracking: 40). Set the fill color for the type (100% Yellow). Set the stroke color to none.

2 Copy the type, then paste it in back (Command-B)[Control-B]. Set the stroke weight to 6 points. You will see the stroke spread. Then set the stroke color (CMYK: 100, 50, 0, 0). You've got the first outline.

3 Repeat Step 2, vary the weight (7 points) and color (black) of the stroke. To complete the effect, I made two more copies with these settings: Second stroke: 13 points (CMYK: 0, 37.5, 75, 0); Third stroke: 15 points (black).

4 Add one more stroke (18 points, black) and use the Left Arrow key to nudge it to the left.

TIP Increasing the stroke weight can sometimes create strange extrusions at the corners of the type outlines. You can alleviate this problem by changing the path Joins to Round. Select the problem type, find the Stroke palette, and click on the middle Join icon (Round).

Gradient Outlines

Illustrator doesn't allow you to fill strokes with gradients, but here is a quick way around that. For more complex gradients on paths see "Path Patterns" (page 134).

1 Enter the text using the Type tool. Choose Type➡Create Outlines. Copy the type. Click on the Swap Fill and Stroke icon on the Tool palette to set the fill color to none and the stroke color to black. Raise the stroke weight a little. I set the stroke weight to 3 points. Don't worry about the stroke color for now.

2 With the type still selected, choose Object➡Path➡Outline Path. This command turns the stroked path into a compound path that is made of two paths that run along the inside and the outside of what used to be the stroke. Essentially, what was a stroke is now a fill. The outlines will thicken a little, but there will be little change onscreen.

3 Simply select a gradient for the fill color. I used the Medium Spectrum gradient from the Color Spectrums file. To access the Color Spectrum gradients choose Window➡Swatch Libraries➡Other Library, then follow this path to find the Spectrums CMYK file: Adobe Illustrator 7.0➡LibrariesGradients➡Spectrums CMYK. The new gradients will appear in a new palette.

115

Offset Outlines

This is an alternate method for creating a thick outline around type that uses the Offset Path command.

I Enter the text (95-point Helvetica Bold) using the Type tool, and choose Type➡Create Outlines. Press (Command-G)[Control-G] to group the type.

2 With the type still selected, choose Object➡Path➡Offset Path. You will have to experiment with how far to offset the path for your type. I offset this type 6 points (Joins: Miter). To be safe, set the Miter limit to the same value as the Offset distance. An expanded copy of the type is placed behind the original.

3 Choose Object➡Pathfinder➡ Unite to clean up this new copy. All of the small corner shapes created by the Offset Path Pathfinder should disappear (actually, they have simply been subsumed into the outline).

4 Fill the expanded outlines with a color or gradient. I used the Steel Blue gradient from the Metal Gradients file (Adobe Illustrator 7.0➡Sample Files➡Gradients➡ Metal Gradients).

5 Select the original type outlines and copy them. Shift the type down one keystroke and to the left one keystroke. Paste a copy of the type in front (Command-F)[Control-F]. Set the fill color for the new copy with a color or gradient. I used the Light Spectrum gradient from the Color Spectrums file (see Step 3 on page 115), and set the stroke color to black (1 point).

6 A shadow completes the type.

VARIATIONS

Complete Steps 1 through 3 (page 114) then follow these steps:

4 Use the Pen tool to draw vertical lines through the letters. If the letter is symmetrical, draw the line in the center of the letter. If not, find a good place for it to run through the type. There are no rules in this step. You can even run several lines through the same letter. Here are the lines I created.

5 Select all of the letters (both copies) and the lines. Choose Object➡Pathfinder➡Divide to separate all of the shapes. Lots of lines, little change. One more step.

6 Set the fill color for all of the selected parts to a linear gradient. Set the stroke color to black, and set the stroke weight to 1 point. Here's the Green Blue preset gradient.

117

Here's the Steel Blue gradient from the Metal Gradients file (see Step 3 on page 115, and open the Metals CMYK file).

Rough Outlines

1 Enter the text using the Type tool. This font is Boton Medium, 110 points. Choose Type➡Create Outlines. Don't worry about the stroke weight and color for now.

2 Make a copy of the type and paste it in back (Command-B) [Control-B]. Click the Swap Fill and Stroke Colors icon on the Toolbar to set the fill color to none and to set the stroke color to black. Raise the stroke weight a little. I set the stroke weight to around 7 points. The appropriate stroke weight will vary with the size of the type.

3 Deselect the copy, and select the original type only. Then choose Object➡Path➡Add Anchor Points. Adding anchor points will give the Roughen filter more points to play with in the next step. Choose Add Anchor points again.

4 Choose Filter➡Distort➡ Roughen. Try these settings for a slightly roughened edge: Size: 3%, Detail: 5/in., Corner.

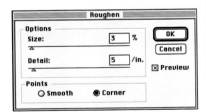

I set the fill color for the rough-ened type to the Waves-Scroll pattern.

Dashed Patterns

Use the Pencil tool to draw some type.

Follow the first four steps on page 114 to create outlines for the type paths. Then press (Command-A) [Control-A] to select all of the type, and (Command-F)[Control-F] to paste a final copy on top. On the Stroke palette, turn on the Dashed Line option. Set the first Dash to 0.1 point and the first Gap to 3 points. Set the stroke weight to 0.5 point. ■

119

Overlapped

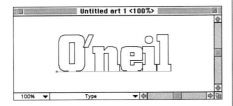

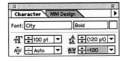

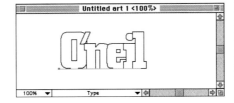

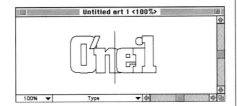

120

TOOLBOX

Extensis
VectorTools

Here are several methods for using the Pathfinders on type that has been…O'lapped.

The Squeeze

1 Enter the text using the Type tool. I used City Bold at 100 points. Set the fill color to white and set the stroke color to black. Because those are the default colors you could either click the default icon or just press D.

2 Find the Character palette and the Tracking box. Set the tracking to a negative number. I set it to −100. You may have to set it even higher. Watch the type squeeze together and overlap.

3 To fine-tune the overlapping letters place the cursor between two letters. Hold down the (Option) [Alt] key and press the Right Arrow key to nudge them apart or the Left Arrow key to nudge them together.

4 One more optional step: Select the type and then choose Type➡ Create Outlines. Then choose Object➡Pathfinder➡Divide. Set the fill color for all to a gradient.

Double O'neils

Set the fill color for the type to a solid color and set the stroke color (2-point stroke) to the same color as the background. Copy the type, paste the copy in back (Command-B) [Control-B], and use the arrow keys to nudge it down and to the left.

Stacked

I Choose Type➡Create Outlines, and set the fill color for the letters to a gradient. Set the stroke weight to 0 (None).

2 Select one letter. Copy it, and paste it in back of that letter only (Command-B)[Control-B]. Set the fill color of the new copy to black. Use the Left Arrow key to nudge the black copy to the left, out from behind the type.

3 Repeat Step 2 for each letter.

121

X-Ray

Choose Type➡Create Outlines, then Object➡Pathfinder➡Divide. Setting the fill color for all to none will make the type see-through. I set the stroke color to white. Copy the type, and paste the copy in back (Command-B)[Control-B]. Shift the copy away from the original using the arrow keys.

Cutout

Choose Type➡Create Outlines, then Object➡Pathfinder➡Exclude. This filter will remove the areas where two letters overlap, allowing you to see through the type.

I placed a filled box behind the type and then another filled box behind that box.

One Letter Only

Skip Step 2 of The Squeeze, choose Type➡Create Outlines, then slide three adjacent letters together. Select only those three letters and choose Object➡Pathfinder➡ Divide. Use the Direct Selection tool to select only the outer parts of the outer letters. Fill the selected parts with a new color.

Unite

After Overlapping the letters, choose Type➡Create Outlines. Then choose Object➡Pathfinder➡ Unite to make the letters all one compound path. A shadow finished it off.

Shifting

Overlap the letters and choose Type➥Create Outlines. Then choose Object➥Pathfinder➥ Divide. Press (Command-Shift-G) [Control-Shift-G]. Choose Object➥Transform➥Transform Each. For this effect, the settings can vary greatly in the dialog box that opens.

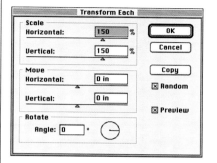

Click OK. I also used the Randomize option on the VectorTools VectorColor palette (Strokes excluded), set the stroke color for all to yellow and added a couple of outlines (page 114). ■

The Area-Type tool enables type to be placed inside any path. Here are a few tips for working with type in paths.

I First, you need an enclosed path. I created this tree image using the Freehand tool.

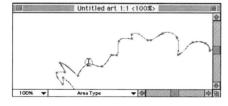

2 Select the Area-Type tool from the Toolbar and click the tool on the edge of the path. The color attributes of the path will disappear and the path will simply become a frame to contain the type.

3 Type away to fill the shape with text. I used Helvetica at 10 points. Watch the point size of the type. If the point size is too large, then the type may not describe the shape with adequate detail. In other words, a large point size could make your tree just look like a blob on the page. (It doesn't, does it?)

4 Type justification is important to this effect. If you want the type to press up against both sides of the path to fill out the shape, select the type, find the Paragraph palette, and click on the Justify Full Lines icon (the fourth icon from the left). If it is only important that the type press against one side or the other, use the Align Left or Align Right mode. The text displayed here is set to Justify Whole Lines. In this example, you can see the difference that justification made in the trunk of the tree.

 TIP **You can edit the path that contains the type at any time, and the type will automatically reflow into the edited path. To select the path only, and not the type,** use the Group Selection tool **and click on the outline path. To select individual points,** use the Direct Selection tool.

Text Wrap

Use the Text Wrap feature to flow type into and around more complicated arrangements. This effect is useful for placing patterned ducks in trees.

1 Create the paths that define the area(s) in which you want to flow type. I want the type to flow into the tree and around the duck.

2 Use the Area Type tool to enter the type into the main path. It will flow underneath or over (depending on which object is in front) the duck.

3 Use the Selection tool to select all of the paths. Choose Type➡Wrap➡Make. The type will flow around the path. The objects have also been grouped. If you want to move only the duck, for example, use the Group Selection tool. Notice also that the duck retained all of its paint style characteristics.

4 You see that the type butts up against the duck. The trick to fixing this problem is creating a larger, invisible duck to use as a wrap to keep the text away from the original duck. Undo back to Step 2. Select the duck and choose Object➡Path➡Offset Path. The amount that the path is offset will become the distance between the duck and the text. I set the offset to 6 points (Joins: Miter). To clean up the new offset path, choose Object➡Pathfinder➡Unite. Set the fill and stroke colors to none.

5 Select the new offset path and the type path. Choose Type➡Wrap➡Make.

TIP To release a text wrap, select the objects and choose Type➡Wrap➡Release.

Holes

Text wraps are the solution to another type-in-a-path problem. Type cannot be flowed into a compound path, and Illustrator will warn you if you try. However, you can fake the effect by using the same Text Wrap technique. Complete Steps 1 through 3, then set the fill and stroke colors of the duck to none.

Linking Paths

You can link two or more paths together so that text flows from one path to the next. Simply select two or more paths and choose Type➡Blocks➡Link. Proceed as in the previous section to enter the text. The type will first flow into the backmost object then continue into the object that is second to the back, and so on. This feature is useful for flowing text from one duck to another.

Linking text blocks automatically groups them. To move only one of the boxes use the Group Selection tool. The paths are also editable as described in the tip on page 125. To unlink the blocks, select any block in the group and choose Type➡ Blocks➡Unlink. All of the blocks will be unlinked and they will all retain the type that they displayed before unlinking them. Bonus: type blocks can be relinked. ∎

You can run type along any path you can create. Because a path can move in almost any direction and create any shape, you can use paths to make your type do flips...really. Now that Illustrator has added the Vertical Path Type tool, your options are even greater.

Along an Object

1 Use the Selection tool to select an object that you want to run type along. I selected the outer path of the dreaded smiley face.

2 Copy the path, and then paste it in front (Command-F)[Control-F].

3 Select the Path Type tool, and move it over the path until the Horizontal bar on the Path Type tool is directly on top of the path. Click on the path.

4 Type in the type. I used Mistral at 32 points.

5 To reposition the beginning of the type, use the Selection tool to grab the I-bar at the beginning of the type. Drag the I-bar along the path in either direction to adjust the starting point of the type.

TOOLBOX

KPT Vector
Effects

6 To raise the type away from the object, activate the Character palette and raise the Baseline Shift. I set the Baseline Shift to 14 points. Watch those pesky descenders.

 If you want to make a change to the path, but not the type on the path, use the Group Selection tool **to select the path. Transform the path as you would any object. The type attributes will not change, and the type will be reflowed onto the transformed path(s).**

The Other Side (of Life)

1 Paste in front (Command-F) [Control-F] the same path that you copied in Step 2 earlier.

2 Again, move the Path Type tool until the horizontal bar on the Path Type tool is directly on top of the path. Click on the path, and enter the text.

129

3 The type is upside down. You can flip the type onto the other side of the path to turn it rightside up. Use the Selection tool to grab the top of the long side of the I-beam, drag the I-beam to the other side of the path. Then drag it along the path to reset the starting point of the text.

4 To shift the type back to the outside of the path (but keep it right-side up), change the Baseline Shift (on the Character palette) to a negative number (−32 points in this case).

5 Final adjustments (of attitude) and shadows for the type.

VARIATIONS

Type on Both Sides of the Same Line

Use the Pen tool to draw a path, and then use the Path Type tool to enter the text (48-point Boton Bold, Tracking: 50).

Use the Selection tool to select the path, and then select the I-beam and drag it to the other side of the path while holding down the (Option)[Alt] key to create an upside down copy of the original path. Some of the type may temporarily disappear because it runs off the path. Don't worry—finish this step to bring it back.

To reposition the type on the path, use the Selection tool to select the path, and then the I-beam. Drag the beam to reposition the starting point of the type.

Use the Type tool to select the type and insert the new text.

I set the fill color of the type and placed boxes behind the type.

Connecting Paths

If you want type to flow from one path to another, you will have to manually cut and paste the type from one path to the next. Create all of the paths first. Then use the Type tool to click and drag a text box. Enter the type into the type box. Press (Command-A)[Control-A] to select all of the type. Copy the type.

Use the Path Type tool to place the text cursor on the first path. Paste in all of the type. You won't see all of the type, but it's all there.

Use the Type tool to place the flashing text cursor after the last complete word on the first path. Press (Command-Shift-Down arrow) [Control-Shift-Down arrow] to select all of the hidden type. Cut the type.

131

the hills into the distance. At the end, a roly-poly man sat as the *period*.

spotted a paragraph unfolding–rolling o

Strolling acroos the landscape, I

Sometimes I feel like I'm always headed in the wrong direction

For many, many years, I could not find the end.

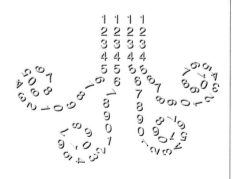

Use the Path Type tool to place the text cursor on the next path. Again, paste in the type. Go back to the previous step. Repeat this process until all of the type has been placed.

Use the Shape Tools

The shape tools make interesting paths for type. I used the Spiral tool to create a path for this type with diminishing point sizes.

Use the Selection tool to select the path and choose Type➡Create Outlines. Choose Filter➡KPT Vector Effects➡Vector Distort and lower the Spherize percentage to –100. I set the fill color of the type with a radial gradient.

Vertical Type

All of the same rules apply for the new vertical type tool. Adjust the Tracking value (on the Character palette) to adjust the vertical space between characters.

Interlocking Paths

Create two paths. Use the Path Type tool to enter the text on each path. Select both paths and choose Type➡Create Outlines. Then choose Object➡Pathfinder➡ Divide. Then press (Command-Shift-G)[Control-Shift-G] to ungroup the divisions. Refer to the "Interlocked" technique (page 90) for instructions on how to complete the Interlocking effect. ■

There is only one path that will take you to the …

There is only one path that will take you to the …

TOOLBOX

PP Template

Path Patterns

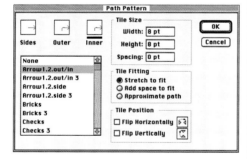

The Path Patterns feature enables you to run patterns along type outlines (or any other path). Four patterns for use on paths are packaged with Illustrator. Try out these patterns, then read "Creating Patterns for Paths" for instructions on how to make your own.

1 Use the Type tool to enter the text. This filter has a difficult time figuring out what to do when the patterns start to run over each other. It's best to use a thick font that leaves some room between the elements of the type. I used Impress at 120 points. Choose Type➡Create Outlines. Set the fill and stroke color to none.

2 Choose Filter➡Stylize➡Path Pattern. Click the Sides icon, then click on Arrow1.2.side 1 in the list below. The object shown in the Sides preview will run along the type outlines. The other two icons show the object that will be placed on the corners of the type outlines. Click the Outer icon, then click the Arrow1.2.out/in 1. Do the same for the Inner icon. Set the Tile Size Width and Height both to around 12 points. Keep it on the Stretch to fit option. The dialog box should look like this.

3 Click OK to see the pattern.

Illustrator is packaged with five other patterns customized for paths, shown from left to right: Dbline, Laurel, Tribevel, Rope, and SolidStar.

VARIATIONS

To mix up the directions of the arrows, drag the Arrow1.2.side icon from the Swatches palette to the image area.

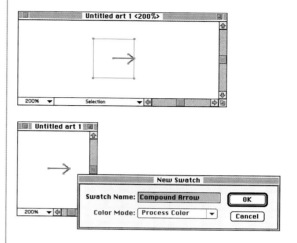

Use the Group Selection tool to deselect the frame and leave only the arrow selected. Choose Object➡Compound Paths➡Make. Shift-Select the empty frame, and choose Edit➡Define Pattern. Name the new pattern "Compound Arrow" when the New Swatch dialog box opens. Delete the arrow and frame.

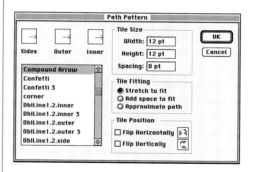

Complete Steps 1 through 3, but use the Compound Arrow file for each of the three icons in the Path Patterns dialog box. Click OK. The arrows will look similar to the way they look in Step 3.

Choose Object➡Transform➡ Transform Each. Turn on the Random and Preview options. Raise the Rotate Angle to around 120°.

135

TIP
Sometimes the pattern will not run completely around the path because the pattern tiles would have to run over each other. If this happens when the pattern is about to run into a corner, then undo the Path Pattern, select the Scissors tool, and click the path near the corner to cut the path. Redo the Path Pattern filter. The pattern should run to the end of the path.

Creating Patterns for Paths

1 Open the PP Template file located on the *Illustrator Type Magic* CD-ROM (ITM Files➡PP Template). This file contains a grid to help you build patterns for paths. Nothing fancy—just a few guides.

2 If you want the pattern to run in a continuous line then the left edge and right edge of the pattern tile must be able to meet. I drew this vine tile using the Pen and Freehand tools. Notice that the vine begins and ends on the same horizontal line.

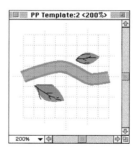

3 Draw a box using the Rectangle tool that stretches from the upper-left corner of the grid to the lower-right corner. Set the fill and stroke color to none. Press (Command-Shift-[)[Control-Shift-[ ] to send the empty rectangle to the back.

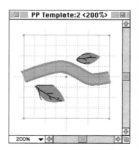

4 Select everything—the empty frame and the pattern tile contents. Choose Edit➡Define Pattern. The New Swatch dialog box opens. Name the swatch "Vine." The Vine pattern can now be found on the Swatches palette.

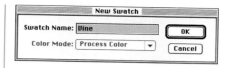

5 Use the Type tool to enter the text. I used Futura ExtraBold at 120 points. Choose Type➡Create Outlines. Set the fill and stroke color to none.

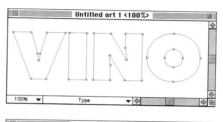

6 In Step 2 on page 134, special patterns were used for the corners in the Path Patterns dialog box. If patterns are not made especially for the corners, then the pattern will break at the corners, and start again on the next path. An alternate method for avoiding this breaking is to round the corners of the path (type outlines). Choose Filter➡ Stylize➡Round Corners (5 points).

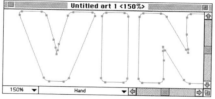

7 Choose Filter➡Stylize➡Path Pattern. Choose the Vine pattern for the Sides, Outer, and Inner icons. Set the Width and Height to 10 points, and match other settings as shown here.

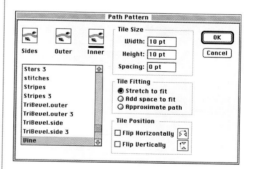

137

Click OK.

VARIATIONS

Open the Path Patterns file on the *Illustrator Type Magic* CD-ROM. This file contains the Vine pattern and several more custom patterns (Illustrator Type Magic➡ITM Files➡Path Patterns). These type examples use the path patterns included on the CD-ROM.

Gradients in Path Patterns

1 Use the Pen tool to draw one short line. Set the stroke color of this line to the beginning gradient color (CMYK: 5, 0, 75, 0). Set the stroke weight to 3 points. The increased stroke weight will help fudge the gaps when the gradient we are creating is snaked along a path.

2 Hold down the Shift and (Option)[Alt] keys as you drag this line to the right. Set the stroke color of the copy to the second gradient (CMYK: 75, 0, 0, 0). Press (Command-D)[Control-D] to make another copy. Set the stroke color to the same color used in Step 1.

3 Select the Blend tool. Click the crosshairs once on the top point of the original line, then (after the dash appears under the crosshairs) click on the top point of the second line.

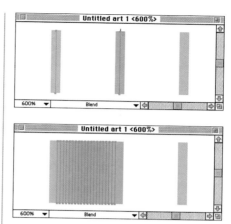

4 Determining the correct number of Steps takes some guesswork. It depends on how far apart the lines are. The resulting lines should be close to each other, and the strokes should definitely be overlapping. I set the Steps to 20. Click OK. The gradient is created by the line of paths created by the Blend tool.

TIP **If there are gaps in the pattern in Step 9, then undo and increase the number of steps in the Blend dialog box in Step 4.**

5 Repeat Steps 3 and 4 to create a gradient between the second and the last line. This is the final gradient.

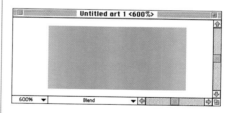

6 Select all of the lines. Choose Edit➡Define Pattern. Name the new pattern "Blend."

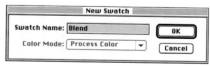

7 Open the PP Template file from the *Illustrator Type Magic* CD-ROM (Illustrator Type Magic➡ITM Files➡PP Template). Use the Pen tool to draw a path like this one on the grid (Stroke weight: 1 point).

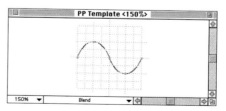

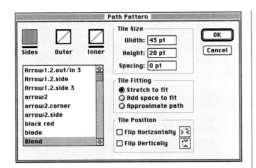

8 Choose Filter➡Stylize➡Path Pattern. Use the Blend pattern for the Sides. Set the Inner and Outer to None. Leave the Tile Size at the default and click OK.

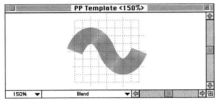

Click OK. This is the pattern for the type.

9 Complete Steps 3 through 8 of the Creating Patterns for Paths section. I named the new pattern S-Blend. Here is the final type.

VARIATIONS

You don't need to put the gradient on a curve. Just complete Steps 1 through 6 of Gradients in Path Patterns, then skip to page 137 and complete Steps 5 through 7 of Creating Patterns for Paths.

The pattern for this path is simply a circle created by the Ellipse tool. After applying the circle as a path pattern, select all and set the fill color to the Yellow/Orange radial gradient. ▪

Here are some techniques to help you work with the basic pattern fills provided by Illustrator. Try them out, then take a look at the Creating Patterns section for instructions on creating your own patterns.

Basic Fill

Use the Type tool to enter the text. Use a font thick enough to display the pattern. I used Highlander at 100 points. Choose Type➡Create Outlines. Click on the pattern button on the bottom of the Swatches palette to display the list of patterns. Click on one of the swatches to fill the type with this pattern. I filled the type with the Polka Dot pattern.

Once you've filled the type with a pattern, there are many variations you can make. Here are some I found.

A Little Twist

When a pattern fill is applied to type, the type outlines are made into a mask for a pattern of objects that extend beyond the borders of the type. An alternate method for filling type with a pattern is to fill a rectangle with the pattern, place the type on top and mask the pattern into the type outlines. It is not as magical as letting Illustrator do the masking for you, but it does allow you to manipulate the pattern fill before applying the mask. After filling the rectangle with a pattern, you can use the Expand Fill command to break the pattern down into the individual objects. Once you have done this, the individual objects can be manipulated to produce a pattern with a little more variety. In this example, the Transform Each feature is used to randomly rotate the individual pieces.

I Use the Type tool to enter the text (100-point Highlander Bold). Choose Type➡Create Outlines. Then Object➡Compound Paths➡ Make to turn the type into a single compound path—which is necessary for the type to act as a mask.

2 Use the Rectangle tool to create a rectangle that covers the type. Fill the rectangle with a pattern. I used the Stars pattern.

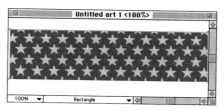

3 Choose Object➡Expand Fill. The clean rectangle will be covered with a web of new guides. The images in the pattern fill have been converted to objects that can be selected and transformed.

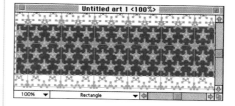

4 Keep everything selected and choose Object➡Masks➡Release. You will see the pattern spread outside of the rectangle. Press (Command-Shift-[)[Control-Shift-[] to send the pattern behind the type.

143

5 Use the Group Selection tool to select one of the background tiles. If the pattern has a transparent background, then a transparent background tile exists behind each group of objects: select one. Choose Edit➡Select➡Same Fill Color. Press Delete to get rid of the tiles. There should also be a second, transparent background tile (if you just deleted it, move on). Repeat this step to get rid of the transparent tiles.

6 Because of the way that many patterns are created, duplicate objects may exist on top of each other. Also some objects in the pattern may be created by two or four parts of the object that combine visually to complete the whole object. Randomly transforming the objects will cause problems because the overlapping or split objects will be transformed differently. To alleviate this problem, select all of the objects in the pattern. Choose Object➡Pathfinder➡ Unite.

7 Keep the objects selected and choose Object➡Transform➡ Transform Each. Turn on the Random and Preview options. Slide the Rotate angle up to about 45°, and set the Horizontal and Vertical Scale percentages to 175%. These settings can vary greatly. Watch the preview and click OK when you find a variation you like.

8 Select everything (Command-A) [Control-A] and choose Object➡Masks➡Make. The pattern, with its added twist, will be comfortably inside the type. Deselect all (Command-Shift-A)[Control-Shift-A].

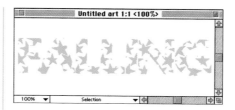

If you know that you will not want to change the pattern fill later, then instead of creating a mask in Step 5, choose Object➡Pathfinder➡Crop. The Crop pathfinder will get rid of all objects (and parts of objects) that do not fall within the type outlines. It will also get rid of the type outlines. If you need the type outlines to create a background fill for example, copy them before applying the Crop pathfinder.

9 To add a background, select the type only and copy it. Select all of the objects (Command-A)[Control-A], and paste the type outlines in back (Command-B)[Control-B]. Set the fill color for the background (Blue, Green, Blue custom gradient).

145

Loosen the Pattern Grid

I filled the type with the same Stars pattern. In Step 6, I used these settings in the Transform Each dialog box:

Which resulted in this:

Which resulted (after completing Steps 5 and 6) in this:

Gradients in Patterns

You can't include a gradient in a pattern that you create, but you can add the gradients after applying the pattern fill to the type.

1 Complete Steps 1 through 6 of "A Little Twist." I used the duck pattern created in "Creating Patterns." Simply fill the objects (the ducks) with a gradient. I chose the Rainbow gradient. With all of the objects selected, I dragged the Gradient tool across all of the objects to make one continuous gradient.

146

2 Create a background and give it the same gradient fill. Use the Gradient tool as in Step 1.

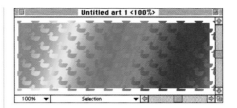

3 You can still do Step 7, if you want. Otherwise, skip ahead and complete Steps 8 and 9.

Patterns in Patterns

All the steps are the same. Fill the ducks with a pattern (Polka Dots). Fill the background with a pattern (Waves-Scroll). I also gave the ducks a 1-point white stroke to set them apart from the background. To add the shadow, copy the ducks and paste them in back (Command-B) [Control-B]. Offset them with the arrow keys, and fill them with black (no stroke).

Transparent Patterns

The duck pattern in the previous figure contains a transparent background. Transparent patterns are great because you can use them to add an extra layer to any type. Select the type outlines, copy them, paste the copy in front, and select the pattern fill. Two more patterns were added to this type.

147

Creating Patterns

These steps will produce a non-random tile pattern. If you want more randomness, then use the "A Little Twist" method for mixing up the pattern after it is created. Before beginning these steps make sure that the Snap to Point option is turned on in the General Preferences (File➡Preferences➡ General).

1 Create the object or group of objects from which you want to create a pattern.

2 Use the Rectangle tool to create a box that will set the tile size. The size of this rectangle, relative to the objects created in Step 1, is impor-tant because it determines the spacing within the pattern. This rectangle is 34 points square. This rectangle will also become the fill color for the pattern. Set the stroke color to none, and set the fill color.

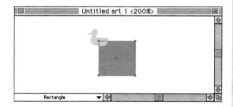

 Patterns cannot contain gradient or pattern fills. Send the rectangle to the back (Command-Shift-[ ) [Control-Shift-[ ].

3 Select the object(s) created in Step 1 and the rectangle created in Step 2. Click the upper-right corner of the rectangle. Hold down the Shift and (Option)[Alt] keys as you drag down to place a new copy directly below the original. Drag until the pointer is directly over the lower-right corner of the original rectangle. When the inside of the arrow turns white, you've hit the right spot.

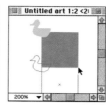 

4 Select both copies of the objects. Hold down the Shift and (Option) [Alt] keys again and click on the lower-left corner of the bottom rectangle. Drag to the right until the pointer is directly over the lower-right corner of the same rectangle. Again, the arrow will turn white when the objects are aligned properly. There should now be four complete sets of the objects.

5 Select and delete the three rectangles just created, but keep the original rectangle and the new objects.

6 Any new objects may be placed on top of the rectangle as long as they do not extend over its edges. I placed another copy of the duck in the center of the rectangle.

Untitled art 1:1 <400%>

400%   Selection

7 Select the original rectangle, copy it, select all (Command-A) [Control-A], and paste the copy in front (Command-F)[Control-F]. Select all of the objects again, and choose Object➡Pathfinder➡Crop. You should now have a trimmed tile ready for patterning. If the objects in the pattern have strokes on them, paste the copy in back, set the fill and stroke colors to none, and go to Step 8. Do not crop the pattern.

> **TIP** To create a pattern with a transparent background, cut the rectangle instead of copying it.

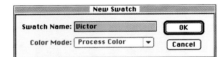

New Swatch

Swatch Name: Victor

Color Mode: Process Color

OK

Cancel

8 Keep the tile selected and choose Edit➡Define Pattern. A dialog box will open allowing you to name the new pattern. I named this new pattern Victor after my cat. The pattern is now complete, and will appear in the list on the Swatches palette.

9 Enter the text using the Type tool (100-point Highlander). Set the fill color to the pattern created earlier.

TIP **Don't forget. Illustrator is packaged with more patterns that do not auto-matically show up in the Swatches palette. To access these patterns, choose Window➥Swatch Libraries➥Other Library and follow this path: Adobe Illustrator 7.0➥Libraries➥ Fill Patterns. Open any of the files to open a new palette of patterns.** ▪

This effect takes advantage of two Illustrator presets—a fill pattern and a gradient. The Random feature in the Transform Each dialog box gives it the final touch.

1 As always, use the Type tool to enter the text. Because of the scale of the pattern that will be used in Step 3, it is necessary to use large point size. Set the point size to about 200, and use a thick typeface like Futura Heavy. It will be easy to scale down the type after finishing the effect. Choose Type➡Create Outlines.

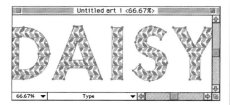

2 While the type is still selected, choose Object➡Compound Paths➡Make. Copy the type.

3 Fill the type with the Laurel.side fill included in the pattern Swatches. This fill pattern is intended for use as a path pattern, but you can still apply it as a fill.

TIP If the petals are too small relative to the type, decrease the point size in Step 1. If the petals are too large, increase the point size.

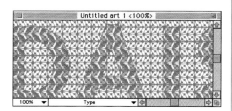

4 Choose Object➡Expand Fill. The edges for all of the individual objects in the fill will show up.

5 Press (Command-Option-7) [Control-Alt-7] to release the mask for the pattern. All of the hidden leaves can now be seen. Press (Command-Shift-G)[Control-Shift-G] to ungroup everything. If you hide the edges (Command-H) [Control-H], all you will see is the Laurel.side pattern.

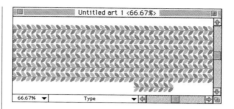

6 Deselect everything (Command-Shift-A)[Control-Shift-A]. There are boxes with fill and stroke colors of none behind the leaves. You can't see them, but use the Selection tool to click around the leaves until you select one. Choose Edit➡ Select➡Same Fill Color. The type outlines will also be selected. Deselect the type outlines. Deselecting one letter will deselect them all because you turned them into a compound path in Step 2. Press Delete to get rid of the empty rectangles.

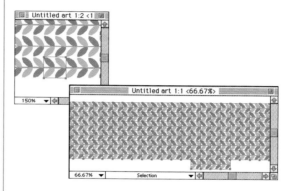

7 Select everything—the type and the leaves and the stems. Choose Object➡Pathfinder➡Crop. All of the leaves outside the type outlines will be removed and the leaves lying on the type outlines will be cut. The leaves will also be grouped.

153

8 Choose Object➡Transform➡ Transform Each. Turn on the Random option. Then set the Horizontal and Vertical Scale percentages both to 160%. Set the Rotate angle to about 70°. Click on the Preview option to test the transformation.

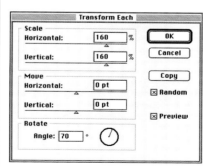

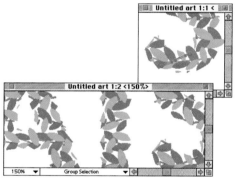

This is the sort of transformation you're looking for.

The Transform Each dialog box is the place to control the density of the petals. For a denser pile of petals increase the Horizontal and Vertical Scale percentages. Lowering these values will open some space between the petals.

9 Deselect everything (Command-A)[Control-A]. Use the Group Selection tool to select one of the stem pieces, then choose Edit➡Select➡Same Fill Color to select all of the stems. Set the fill color of the stems to a green (CMYK: 50, 10, 85, 15).

10 Hold down the Shift key and drag a selection over all of the type. The green stems will be deselected and the petals will be selected. Set the fill color to the Yellow & Orange Radial gradient found on the Swatches palette. Set the stroke color to CMYK values: 10, 0, 70, 3, and set the stroke weight to 0.5 points. The petals are complete. Complete Step 11 if you want to add a shadow.

154

II Select All, and copy all. Then paste a copy in back (Command-B) [Control-B] for a shadow. Press (Command-G)[Control-G] to group the shadow objects. Set the fill color to black. Then use the arrow keys to shift the shadow down and to the left. Here's a detail of the effect, followed by the full image.

TIP

To scale the type down to the size you want to use it, select all (Command-A) [Control-A] and double-click the Scale tool. Set the scale percentage and turn on the Scale line weight option so that the stroke weight on the petals is properly reduced.

VARIATIONS

Other colors will also work. I changed the gradient colors directly on the Gradient palette. ■

155

This book focuses on type effects that are created solely within Illustrator. Many times however, the type effect you are looking for cannot be fully achieved through the use of Illustrator's features alone. Fortunately, Illustrator works well with some other applications, and it works especially well with Photoshop. The techniques that follow are a taste of what combining the features of these two applications can produce.

Type on Paths in Photoshop

There are several ways that Illustrator and Photoshop can trade information. Perhaps the easiest way is to have both applications open at the same time. Then objects can be dragged from an open Illustrator window to an open Photoshop window, and vice versa. You must have Photoshop 4.0 to perform this drag and drop procedure.

Both Illustrator and Photoshop can now handle vector and raster grahics. However, Photoshop is primarily a raster graphics application and therefore has limited vector grahics capabilities. Illustrator has limited raster graphics capabilities. Graphics can be traded back and forth, but what you can do with them in each application will depend on the type of graphic that is being used.

1 Illustrator is better at arranging type. See "On Paths" (page 128) to find out how to put type on a path (MetaPlusBlack, 50 points). Then convert the type to outlines (Type➡Create Outlines).

2 With the Illustrator window still open, launch Photoshop and open a new file (Command-N)[Control-N] (4×2 inches, 300 ppi, RGB).

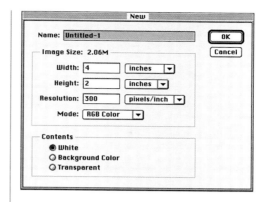

3 Return to the Illustrator file, select the objects to be used in Photoshop, and drag them across the screen and onto the open Photoshop window. When the arrow is over the Photoshop window, a gray square will run around the inside border of the window. Release the mouse to drop the objects into Photoshop. They will be automatically placed into a new layer (Layer 1).

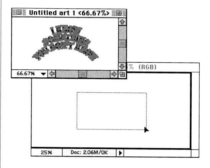

4 Click on the Photoshop window to activate it. Hold down the (Command)[Control] key and click on Layer 1 in the Layers palette to load the selection of Layer 1. Choose Select➡Save Selection (click OK to accept the default settings) to create Channel #4. Click on Channel #4 on the Channels palette to activate it.

5 The selection should still be active. Choose Filter➡Blur➡ Guassian Blur (5 pixels). If you are using a lower ppi, then lower the Blur amount proportionately. This command will blur the inside of the type only.

6 Return to the composite (RGB) channel (Command-~)[Control-~]. Choose a color for the type color (CMYK: 0, 85, 75, 0), then press (Option)[Alt]-Delete to fill the type with the new color.

7 Choose Filter➞Render➞Lighting Effects. Match the settings in that big fancy dialog box to what you see in this figure. The light color is CMYK: 20, 0, 65, 0.

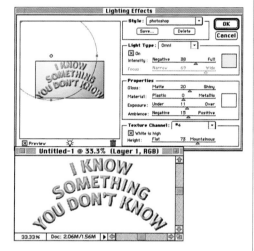

8 To add the shadow, activate the Background layer, choose Select➞ Feather (5 pixels). Choose a color for the shadow and press (Option) [Alt]-Delete to fill the shadow selection with the new color. Select the move tool and use the arrow keys to shift the shadow away from the type.

| TIP | **Alternately, you can copy paths from either Photoshop or Illustrator and paste them into the other application. You can also save Photoshop paths as Illustrator files (File➞Export➞Paths to Illustrator). Photoshop can open Illustrator files. You can also export Illustrator** |

files as Photoshop 4 files
(File➡Export). Finally,
Photoshop files can be
placed (File➡Place) as
complete objects into
Illustrator (see "Masked,"
page 104 for more on placing files). Enough?

Embers

1 Use the Type tool to enter the
text (Futura ExtraBold at 100
points). Choose Type➡Create
Outlines. Press (Command-8)
[Control-8] to turn the type into
a single compound path.

2 Here is a quick way to make
stripes in type. Set the fill color of
the type with any gradient (Black,
White gradient), then choose
Object➡Expand Fill. The number of
steps that you enter in the Expand
dialog box will be the number of
steps in the type. I chose 100 steps.

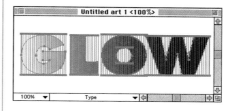

3 Choose Object➡Pathfinder➡
Crop to release the masked stripes
and crop them into the type outlines all in one step.

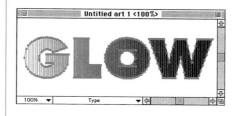

4 Choose Object➡Transform➡
Transform Each, and raise the
Rotate Angle to about 35°. Turn on
the Random option and click OK.

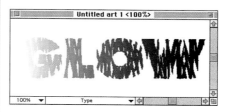

5 Set the fill color for all to the Black, White gradient to complete the Illustrator part of this type treatment.

6 Choose File➡Export. Choose Photoshop 4 from the Format pop-up menu. Name the file (Glow.ps4) and save it. Quit Illustrator.

7 Launch Photoshop, and open the file saved in the previous step. Choose Image➡Mode➡Grayscale (OK to discard color information). Then choose Filter➡Brush Strokes➡Accented Edges (Edge Width: 3, Edge Brightness: 8, Smoothness: 12).

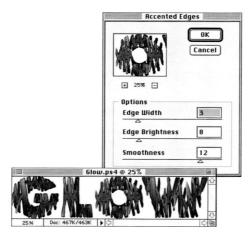

8 Choose Image➡Mode➡Indexed Color, then Image➡Mode➡Color Table. From the pop-up menu choose Black Body.

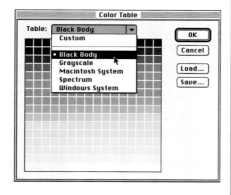

Click OK to see the type transformed. ■

Some of Illustrator's filters can only be used on rasterized images. They are essentially Photoshop filters. By rasterizing type outlines, you can create Photoshop-like effects right in Illustrator. The following pages show a few effects which are aided by the Rasterize feature. Many of these filters will work only on rasterized RGB images. Remember, once you have rasterized an object, it cannot be converted back into objects.

Rasterized Type Outlines

I Use the Type tool to enter the text. I used Garamond at 90 points. Use the Selection tool to select the type, and copy it. No need to convert the type to outlines; type can be rasterized directly.

2 Use the Rectangle tool to draw a rectangle around the type. It needs to be only slightly larger than the type. Set the fill color to white and set the stroke color to none. Press (Command-Shift-[)[Control-Shift-[ ] to send the white rectangle behind the type. The rectangle will add a border to the rasterized type that will allow the halftone to expand in Step 4.

3 Select the type and the rectangle, and choose Object➡Rasterize to open the Rasterize dialog box. The proper settings will depend on your needs. Higher resolution means higher quality and finer detail, but it also means the file will need more time and more RAM to rasterize. I chose the Medium Resolution option (150 ppi). Choose a color mode from the pop-up menu. As stated above, many filters will only work on images rasterized into RGB mode. For this effect, choose RGB.

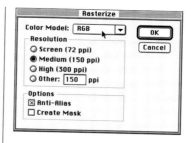

You will see little change in the type. The edges will get a little softer, but most importantly, you can now only select the type as a complete box. The areas inside the box, but outside the type, will be filled with white. If you need this area to be transparent, then undo and turn on the Mask option in the Rasterize dialog box.

4 Choose Filter➡Pixelate➡Color Halftone to open the Color Halftone dialog box. Click the defaults button to reset all values. Click OK. ■

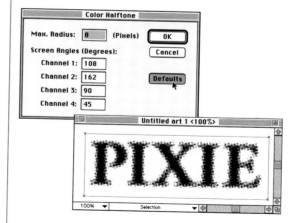

5 Press (Command-F)[Control-F] to paste a copy of the type outlines in front of the halftone image. Set the fill color to white and set the stroke color to none.

Before saving the file for output, convert the rasterized type to CMYK mode. Select the rasterized image only and choose Filter➡ Colors➡Convert to CMYK. If you don't, then when saving the file you will receive a message warning you about possible printing problems. If the type is only intended for screen display, then this step is unnecessary.

Rasterized Objects

Use Rasterize to aid in creating a fill for type outlines.

I Use the Rectangle tool to create a rectangle that can hold the type. Select the Knife tool. Click the rectangle and drag many times back and forth across it. If you have KPT VectorEffects installed then choose Filter➡KPT Vector Effects➡KPT ShatterBox instead of using the Knife tool. Use the Random Lines or Random Curves feature.

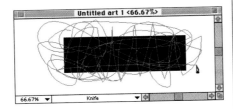

2 Choose a variety of colors for the individual shapes within the rectangle, or select them all and click the Randomize color button on the VectorTools VectorColor palette.

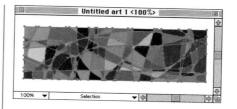

3 Choose Object➡Rasterize and choose the settings. Make sure to choose RGB as the color mode.

4 Use the Type tool to enter text directly on top of the colored image (105-point AGaramond). Choose Type➡Create Outlines and Object➡Compound Paths➡Make to convert all of the type into a single compound path.

5 Select the type outlines and the rasterized image and choose Object➡Mask➡Make. Creating the type mask now will allow you to see how the filter effects look inside of the type.

6 Deselect all (Command-Shift-A) [Control-Shift-A], then select the rasterized image only. You can now experiment with the filters to create some unique fills. I used three filters in this example. Choose Filter➡Texture➡Patchwork (Square Size: 4, Relief: 8) to separate the random areas of color into groups of tiles.

7 Choose Filter➡Texture➡Grain (Intensity: 75, Contrast: 55, Grain Type: Regular) to make the tiles appear a little weathered.

8 For the last filter, choose Filter➡Blur➡Radial Blur (Amount: 50, Spin, Good) to smear the colors with a circular motion.

9 Select the mask type outlines, and copy them. You can paste in copies of these type outlines for adding a stroke and shadow. If you intend to print this image, then select the rasterized image, and choose Filter➡Colors➡Convert to CMYK.

Rasterized Images

The same filters can also be applied to raster images that have been imported into Illustrator. The advantage of applying filters in Illustrator is the capability to undo multiple filters. Photoshop is limited to only one undo. To import an image, choose File➡Place. Follow the previous steps to complete the effect. I applied the Distort➡Glass (Distortion: 9, Smoothness: 3, Texture: Tiny Lens, Scaling: 177) and the BrushStrokes➡Accented Edges (Edge Width: 2, Edge Brightness: 39, Smoothness: 3) filters to this image before masking it into type outlines.

 TIP **If the imported image is a CMYK image, then you can quickly convert it to RGB mode by choosing Filter➡Colors➡Convert to RGB.** ■

Wrap a ribbon around type with the aid of the Pathfinders in the Object menu.

1 Use the Type tool to enter the text. I think a serif typeface looks good with this effect. The serifs give you a few extra crevices to tuck the ribbon around. I used Matrix Bold at 96 points. Choose Type➡Create Outlines. Then choose Object➡Compound Paths➡Make. This last step is necessary in order to make the Intersect pathfinder work correctly in Step 4.

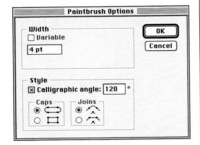

2 Double-click the Paintbrush tool to open the Brush dialog box. Here you can set the characteristics of the paint strokes. The Width will be the height of the ribbon. I set it to 4 points. If you've got a pressure-sensitive tablet then play with the Variable settings. The rest of us will settle for the Calligraphic option. Turn it on, and set the angle to 120°.

3 With one long click and drag I drew this ribbon wrapping around the type, then set the fill color to a gradient.

4 Select the type and the ribbon, copy them, then paste them in front (Command-F)[Control-F]. Choose Object➡Pathfinder➡Intersect. This filter will leave only the small areas of type where the ribbon and type overlap. Set the fill color to the same color as the type fill color and ungroup them (Command-Shift-G)[Control-Shift-G]. Press (Command-Shift-A)[Control-Shift-A] to deselect them.

5 Decide where the ribbon will run over the type and where it will run under the type. Select the small pieces created in Step 4 that are on top of the points at which the ribbon will run over the type. Press Delete to get rid of them.

TIP Some small pixels may show through at the edges where the small pieces of type were pasted on top of the ribbon. Use the Direct-Selection tool to pull the points of the small pieces of type over the peeking ribbon.

169

VARIATIONS

Gradient

If you want to run a gradient through the type also, then select the type and all of the remaining small pieces. Do not select the ribbon. Choose the gradient fill and use the Gradient tool to direct the gradient through the type. Using the Gradient tool will unite all of the pieces to look as if they are one.

Shadow

If you want to cast the shadow of the ribbon onto the type, then select the ribbon and the type (but not the small pieces), copy them and paste them in front (Command-F)[Control-F]. Select the ribbon copy only and move it by pressing the Down and Right arrow keys each once. Fill the ribbon copy with black.

Shift select the type copy, then choose Object➡Pathfinder➡ Intersect. Only shadows remain.

Cut the shadows, select the ribbon, and paste them in back (Command-B)[Control-B].

But there are shadows in places we don't want them. Sorry, you'll have to get rid of them the old-fashioned way. First, ungroup them (Command-Shift-F)[Control-Shift-G]. Then use the Selection tool to select the stray shadows and delete them.

Masking the Type

It is difficult to fill the type with anything but a solid fill or a gradient because the type exists on two separate levels—the type outlines in the background and the small intersecting pieces on top of the ribbon. If you want to use the type outlines as a mask (or a pattern fill), then before Step 4 place the type on top of the ribbon. After applying the Intersect pathfinder in Step 4, fill the intersections with the ribbon color (or gradient). If the ribbon is filled with a gradient, then select the ribbon and all of the intersections and use the Gradient tool to redirect the gradient. This will unite (visually) the ribbon and the intersections. The type outlines can now safely be used as a mask. I masked in this texture created with the Ink Pen filter. ■

KPT Vector
Effects

For this effect, you will first use the Blend tool to set up a palette of blended strokes. By layering copies of type and transferring the paint style attributes of each of the blended strokes to the type outline copies, an illusion of roundness is formed.

1 Use the Pen tool to draw a short, vertical line. Set the stroke color to the interior (highlight) color for the type. I used CMYK values: 25, 12.5, 0, 0. Set the stroke weight to 1 point, and set the fill color to none.

2 Drag a copy (hold down the (Option)[Alt] key while dragging) of the line to the right a short distance. Set the stroke weight of the copy to 8 points and set the stroke color to the color for the exterior (base) of the type. I used CMYK: 75, 43, 0, 0. Set the fill color to none.

3 Select both lines and select the Blend tool. Click once on the top point of the original line, then (after the dash appears below the crosshairs) click once on the top point of the second line. This tells Illustrator that as the first object is blended toward the second object, the first point clicked will move toward the second point clicked. In this case, the points are directly in line with each other, so the top points of all of new lines created by the Blend tool will line up with each other at the same vertical position, and the bottom points will just follow along.

4 A dialog box will appear asking you how many steps you want to create between the two lines. The number of steps needed for your type depends on the size of the type. Be careful not to use so few that the final gradation is not smooth. I chose 10 steps for this 65-point type. After clicking OK, you have completed the template for your type.

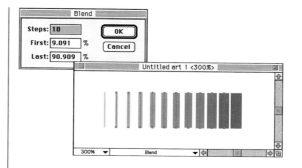

5 Enter the text using the Type tool. This technique does not fill the interior; it uses the type outlines. Therefore, it will work best if you use a thick font that has some space between the paths. I used Thickhead at 65 points. Choose Type➥Create Outlines. Copy the type.

6 Select the Eyedropper tool and double-click on the thinnest line of the blended template lines. This will transfer the Paint Style attributes of the template line to the type outline path.

7 Paste a copy of the type in back (Command-B)[Control-B]. Then, keep repeating Steps 6 and 7 until you have pasted one copy of the type for each of the template lines.

8 A final copy of the type, still filled with black will remain. Set the fill color of the type to none, and set the stroke color to black. Set the stroke weight of the type to the same as the thickest line (8 points). This extra outline will strengthen the edges. I shifted it away from the type—down and to the left.

VARIATIONS

Dashed Lines

Select all of the stacked type copies and play with the Dashed Line settings at the bottom of the Paint Style palette. The settings I used for each of these examples are listed beside each figure.

Select all copies of the type (except the shadow) and turn on the Dashed Line option. Set the first Dash to 4 points and the first Gap to 4 points. Change the Cap to Projecting and the Join to Round.

Select all copies of the type (except the shadow) and turn on the Dashed Line option. Set the first Dash to 0.1 point and the first Gap to 6 points. Change the Cap to Round and the Join to Round.

Select all copies of the type (except the shadow) and turn on the Dashed Line option. Set the first Dash to 4 points and the first Gap to 4 points. Change the Cap to Butt and the Join to Round. A gap will be created between the dashes.

PAY

MORE

PLEASE

Select all of the type outlines
and paste another copy in back
(Command-B)[Control-B]. Set the
stroke color to the color of the
thickest line and keep the dash
solid so it fills in the gaps. I also set
the fill color (CMYK: 75, 70, 0, 0); it
became the fill color for the type.

Blended Outlines

You can also make multicolor gradients with this technique. If the colors are far enough apart then the
type will look like it has blended
multicolor outlines. Here are the
template lines I used. I used the
Blend tool on the first and fifth
lines. Then I used it again on the
fifth and ninth lines.

And the type turned out like this.

KPT ColorTweak

If the blended round border of
your type turns out a little dull...

... then select all of the copies of
the type and choose Filter➡KPT
Vector Effects➡KPT ColorTweak.
Raise the Contrast to the maximum (100%) to brighten the
type. ■

One of the simplest operations in Illustrator, scaling can do wonders for type. Here are a few effects to try.

For each effect, I used the Type tool to enter text.

Diminishing Scale

Select each letter and change the point size. These letters range from 12 to 100 points.

Diminishing Scale Distorted

Use the type from the previous example and choose Type➤Create Outlines. Then choose Filter➤ Distort➤Free Distort. Slide the lower-right corner straight upwards.

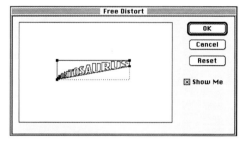

You should get something like this.

Select the Rotate tool, set the orientation point at the lower-left corner of the type, then swing the type down. I added a white stroke and an offset shadow.

176

Horizontal Scale

Choose Type➡Create Outlines,
select each letter individually, and
use the Scale tool to scale each.
Hold down the Shift key and scale
the letters in the horizontal direction only. Then squeeze them
together, change their colors, and
add a drop shadow.

Varying Scale

Choose Type➡Create Outlines and
use the Scale tool to play with scale
and letter shapes.

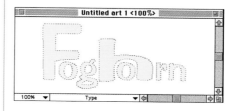

Scaling Parts

Have fun scaling parts of letters.
Choose Type➡Create Outlines,
then use the Knife tool to cut
across the feet of your serif
(Garton at 85 points) type.

Choose Filter➡Distort➡Free
Distort and spread the two bottom
points down and apart.

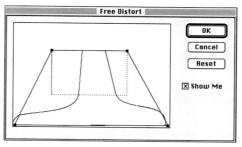

Do this to each of the feet. I re-applied the filter (Command-E) [Control-E] to some of the feet to add variation.

Rising Scale

Begin with a small copy of the type (Cochin, 100 points). Select the Scale tool, then hold down the (Option)[Alt] key and click to the left of the type, along the imaginary baseline.

The Scale dialog box will appear onscreen. Select Non-Uniform from the pop-up menu. Then set the Horizontal scale value to 102% and the Vertical scale value to 104%. Click Copy.

Press (Command-D)[Control-D] to continue making scaled copies of the type. I made 11 copies. Set the fill color of all copies to none, set the stroke color to black, and set the stroke weight to one point. Then set the fill color of the top copy to a yellow.

Random Scale

Choose Type➡Create Outlines. Choose Edit➡Transform Each. Turn on the Random and Preview options. Here are the settings I used, but this one-stepper is crying for experimentation. Horizontal Scale: 124%, Vertical Scale: −10%, Horizontal Move: 10, Vertical Move: −10. Keep turning the Random option on and off to see different variations.

I slid them together, selected them all and chose Object➡Pathfinder➡ Unite.

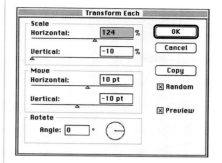

Stretched Scale

Choose Type➡Create Outlines (Impact, 60 points). Then use the Direct Selection tool to drag a selection box around the bottom portion of the letters, like this.

Examine the selected points. Letters with curved bottoms may cause some trouble. For those letters you want to be sure that the topmost point selected is at the bottom of a true-vertical segment of the type outline. See the selections I made here.

After you've got the right points selected, use the Direct Selection tool to drag the bottoms down. You will know immediately if you've made a mistake in selecting points in the previous step. If so, press (Command-Z)[Control-Z] to fix the selection, and try moving the points again. Here's what your text should look like.

Follow the same procedure and rules for the tops of the letters.

I gave the letters a gradient fill and shadow.

The same technique works in the Horizontal direction, and is a little easier because you only have two letters to worry about.

You can't scribble on the walls at home, but you can in Illustrator. You can create some cool effects with the Pencil tool.

1 Do not use the Type tool to enter the text. Do not even select the Type tool. Instead select the Pencil tool. Set the fill color to none and set the stroke color to any color you want. Set the stroke weight to 1 point.

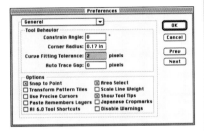

2 Choose File➡Preferences➡ General. The Preferences dialog box contains a Curve Fitting Tolerance setting. The higher the number the less precise and smoother the line you draw with the Pencil tool will be. A high setting will take the jitters out of the line. A low setting will reproduce your exact movements. 2 pixels is a good balance.

3 Use the mouse like a pencil to draw some type. Pretty simple. Draw the type about three times the size that you want to use it.

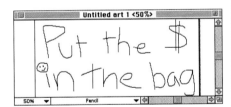

TIP If you have a pressure-sensitive pen for your drawing tablet, this is a great place to use it.

4 Then use the Scale tool to shrink the type back down again. The shrinking is an old trick that will hide minor flaws in the lines.

VARIATIONS

Circling

Try moving in a circular pattern as you write the letters and words.

More Color

Select all of the type, copy it, and paste a copy in front (Command-F)[Control-F]. Turn on the Dashed Line option. I set the first Dash and Gap both to 12. Set the stroke color (CMYK 53, 15, 78, 22).

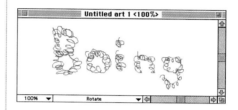

Paste more copies in front, setting the stroke color and Dashed Line settings for each.

Paintbrush

Instead of the Pencil tool, double-click the Paintbrush tool to select it and open the Brush dialog box. Turn on the Calligraphic option. Try an angle of 120°. Set the stroke weight to about 4 points. Set the fill color to a color for the type and then set the stroke color to none.

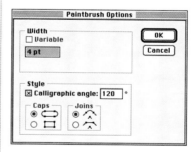

Draw the type as in the first Scribble technique to produce an inked line.

TIP	**After drawing a line with the pen tool, choose Object➡Pathfinder➡Unite to simplify the path and help clean it up a little.**

183

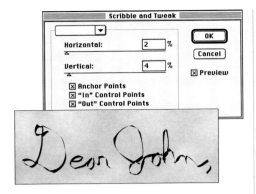

For messy ink, follow the previous variation, then choose Filter➡ Distort➡Scribble and Tweak. Keep the settings low (Scribble, Horizontal: 2, Vertical: 4).

> **TIP** Turning the Preview option on and off in the Scribble and Tweak dialog box will produce random variations with the same settings.

If you use the Pencil tool to create the type, then you can apply some of the other effects in this book to that path.

Rounded

This Pencil path…

…becomes this type after applying the "Rounded" effect (page 172) and adding a shadow.

184

More

See page 84 to find out about the Ink Pen filter.

See "Shaggy" (page 204) for this sketchy effect.

Try the KPT Vector Sketch filter. Select the type outline paths and choose Filter➟KPT Vector Effects➟KPT Sketch. ▪

Illustrator has a tough time making blended shadows. This technique, which resembles the Rounded technique (page 172), allows you to blend the shadow from any shadow color to any background color. You can also move the shadow in any direction after creating it. The second method, which uses the Drop Shadow filter, is great for quick blends, but is not quite as versatile because once you have created the shadow to shift away from the type in a certain direction, you cannot move it. You would have to delete and then re-create it to shift away in the new direction.

1 Use the Pen tool to draw a short, vertical line. Set the stroke color to the darkest color for the shadow (CMYK: 30, 30, 30, 100) and then set the fill color to none. Set the stroke weight to 1 point.

2 Select the line with the Selection tool, then hold down the Shift and (Option)[Alt] keys as you drag the line to the right. Set the stroke color for the copied line to the color of the background behind the type. The thickness of the shadow blend will be equal to half of the stroke weight of this line. I set the stroke weight to 10 points.

3 Select both lines, then select the Blend tool. Click once on the top of the original line, then click once on the top of the copied line.

4 The Blend dialog box will open. The number of Steps will determine the smoothness of the shadow blend. Match this setting to the width of the second line—10 points.

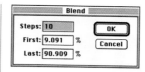

These lines created by the Blend command act as a palette for creating the blended shadow. Keep these lines in the image window, but set them out of the way.

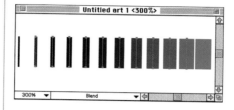

5 Use the Type tool to enter the text (Machine at 90 points) and choose Type➡Create Outlines. Copy the type. If you are placing this shadow behind existing type, select the type outlines. Then select all other parts of the type and press (Command-U)[Control-U] to hide them temporarily. It is easier to see what's going on in this technique if the type is out of the way. Only the type outlines that will define the general shape of the shadow should be visible.

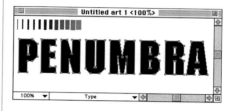

6 Choose Object➡Path➡Offset Path to open the Offset dialog box. The shadow will be improved if the type outlines for the shadow are slightly smaller than the outlines for the real type. Set the Offset distance to −3 points (Joins: Miter; Miter Limit: 1).

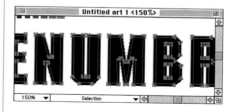

187

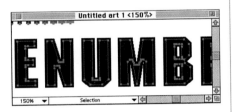

7 It is likely that a few odd shapes were created at the corners of the type by the Offset command. While the offset type is still selected, choose Object➡Pathfinder➡ Divide, then press (Command-Shift-G)[Control-Shift-G] to ungroup the divided pieces. Use the Selection tool to deselect the central offset type so that only the small corner pieces remain selected. Don't forget to deselect the paths that create the holes in letters like P's and B's. Press Delete to get rid of the paths.

I selected the remaining offset type outlines to show what should be left after deleting the corner pieces.

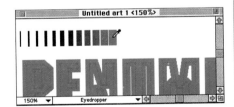

8 Also, select the original type outlines and press (Command-U) [Control-U] to temporarily hide them. The only remaining visible parts of the type are the shrunken offset copies.

9 Select the shrunken type and copy it. Get the Eyedropper tool, find the palette of lines created in Step 4, and double-click the Eyedropper on the thickest line— the one colored with the background color. The type outlines will take on the attributes of the line from the palette. If you are working on a background of the same color as the shadow background color, you won't be able to see it because the stroke color matches the background color.

10 Press (Command-F)[Control-F] to paste a copy of the type in front. Use the Eyedropper tool again, and click on the next thickest line in the palette. Repeat this step until a copy of the type has been created for each line in the palette. The shadow will blend gradually as you apply the palette line attributes.

11 When the last copy is still selected, set the fill color to the same as the stroke color—the darkest color for the shadow. You now have the shadow. Select all of the shadow type outlines (which are stacked directly on top of each other and therefore display only one edge) by dragging a marquee over them with the Selection tool. Group them (Command-G) [Control-G].

 TIP This technique produces a shadow with sharp corners. If you want rounded corners, then after selecting all of the shadow copies, click the Round icon for the Join on the Stroke palette.

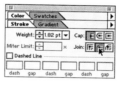

12 Once the blended shadow is moved onto its background, you see the blend working.

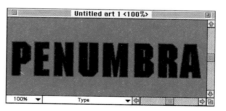

189

13 Press (Command-Shift-U) [Control-Shift-U] to reveal the original type. Right now the shadow is directly under the type. Select the shadow only, or the type only, and use the arrow keys to shift them away from each other slightly.

Drop Shadow Filter

The Drop Shadow filter essentially pastes a copy of the selected object behind the original. At the same time, it offsets the copy a predetermined distance, and adjusts the percentage of black in the fill and stroke colors. Because it does all that in one step, you can use it to quickly create blended shadows.

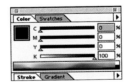

1 Use the Type tool to enter the text or the shape that will be used for the shadow. I used Freehand521 at 110 points. If you want, raise the Tracking value to create some space between the letters for the shadows to fit. Choose Type➡ Create Outlines.

2 Setting the fill color in this technique is very important. Make sure that the color mode is set to CMYK. Set the fill color to the same as the background color (white in this example), and then raise the K value to darken the shadow. I set the K value at 100% (CMYK: 0, 0, 0, 100). Set the stroke color to none, and copy the type.

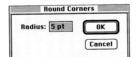

3 Choose Filter➡Stylize➡Round Corners. The appropriate Radius will vary with the size of your type. I set the Radius to 5 points, but this type did not need much rounding because most of its corners were already rounded.

4 Choose Filter➡Stylize➡Drop Shadow. Use the settings shown in the figure (.25, .2, –5%). The Intensity setting is actually the percentage change of K (as in CMYK) for the shadow color. Therefore, if the K value of the original shadow created in Step 1 was 100%, then the K value of the first copy will be 95%. You won't see much of a change because the offset and color changes are so slight, but you will notice a slight shift of the type.

5 Press (Command-E)[Control-E] to repeat the filter. Do this 18 more times, or until the fill color turns white.

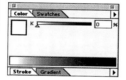

TIP You can watch the fill color percentage box on the Color palette to know for certain when the fill color reaches white (0% black(K)). If the fill color becomes the same color as the background color too quickly, then lower the Intensity percentage in Step 3, perhaps to –4%or –3%.

6 Select all, and press (Command-F) [Control-F] to paste the original type in front of the shadow. Set the fill and stroke colors and you're done.

191

Shadows

Funky Blends

1 Use the Type tool to enter the text. I used Helvetica Compressed at 110 points. Choose Type➡ Create Outlines.

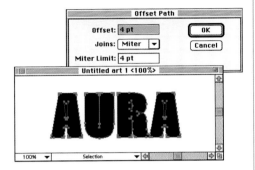

2 Choose Filter➡Objects➡Offset Path. In the dialog box set the Offset to 4 points to enlarge the type. This amount may vary depending on the size of the type. Set the Joins to Miter, and the Miter Limit to 4 points—the same as the Offset distance.

3 Choose Filter➡Pathfinder➡ Unite to unite the odd shapes that formed in the corners of the type. Press (Command-Shift-G)[Control-Shift-G] to ungroup the letters.

4 Press (Command-Shift-[) [Control-Shift-[ ] to send the expanded type to the back. Set the fill color to white, and set the stroke color to none. Select the original type in front again, and copy it.

5 Select the Blend tool, and then select both copies of the first letter. Click on one point of the original (inner) type outlines, then after the dash appears below the crosshairs, click on one point of the expanded type outlines. Do not be concerned about letters that include compound paths—that helps create the odd shadow shapes.

6 After clicking on the second point, the Blend dialog box will open. Set the number of Steps to 10, and click OK to see the blend for the first letter.

7 Repeat Steps 5 and 6 for each letter. As you proceed from one letter to the next, use points on various sides of the letters. Here are the blends for the rest of the letters.

8 To finish this effect, select all and paste the original type in front (Command-F)[Control-F]. Try setting the fill color to white and setting the stroke color to none.

Or, fill them with the Steel Bar gradient and use the Gradient tool to direct the gradient. ■

193

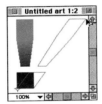

194

Receding Shadows

1 Use the Type tool to enter the text (100-point Helvetica Condensed Black). Choose Type➡ Create Outlines. I scaled each character individually. I set the fill color of all of them to the Green, Blue gradient.

2 Select one of the letters. Select the Shear tool. Click once to set the axis point for the Shear tool at the lower-left corner of the type.

3 Then click the type and drag it to the right while holding down the Shift and (Option)[Alt] keys. This will place a sheared copy in front of the original. The distance that you shear the type determines how far the shadow reaches to the right. We will set the depth in the next two steps. Cut the sheared copy, select the original and paste the copy in back (Command-B) [Control-B]. Don't worry about the color of the shadow. We'll fix that later.

4 Keep the sheared copy selected and select the Scale tool. Set the Scale axis point at the bottom center of the character.

5 Click the pointer near the top of the sheared type and drag downward while holding down the Shift key. That is the basic shape of the shadow.

6 This step is optional, but will add a little perspective to the shadow to make it look as if it is truly receding in space. Choose Filter➡ Distort➡Free Distort, and move the two top corners of the distort box only. If you move the bottom corners, then the shadow baseline will not match up with baseline of the type. Try something like this...

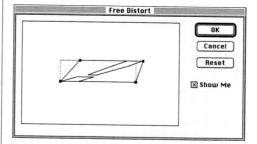

...to get this.

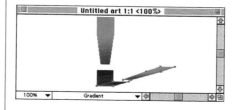

7 Set the fill color to the Black, White gradient. Select the Gradient tool and hold down the Shift key as you click and drag from the top of the shadow toward, and past, the baseline of the type.

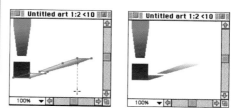

195

8 Repeat all steps for all characters.

VARIATIONS

Sometimes reversing the direction of the shadows gradient fill is desirable. Click and drag from the bottom up while holding down the Shift key in Step 7.

See page 246 in the "Transparent" technique for instructions on how to put this shadow on a background.

Leaning Type

1 Enter the text using the Type tool. I made the point size of each letter slightly larger than the preceding the letter. Choose Type➡ Create Outlines. Set the fill color to the Black, White gradient—this will be the shadow. Use the Gradient tool to direct the gradient straight upward for each letter.

2 Then select the Shear tool and set the orientation point at the lower-left of the type.

3 Hold down the Shift and (Option)[Alt] keys while dragging to the left from the upper-left corner of the type.

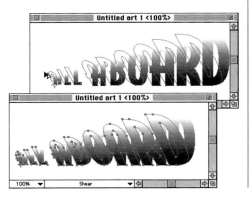

4 Set the fill color to the Yellow & Purple Radial gradient. I selected each letter one at a time and dragged the Gradient tool from the bottom-center upward.

5 As a final touch, I double-clicked the Rotate tool and rotated the type −15°. ∎

Here are four ways to make quick shadows.

Copy and Paste

1 If you are starting from scratch then use the Type tool to enter the text. There is no need to convert the type to outlines. Select the type baseline. If you want to put a shadow behind existing type, then select the outlines of the type for use as a form for the shadow.

2 To make a quick drop shadow, copy the selection, select all objects that are part of the type and paste the copy in back (Command-B) [Control-B]. Use the arrow keys to offset the copy. Then set the fill color to black or another color for the shadow.

VARIATION

The advantage of converting the type to outlines is that you have more fill options. You can't fill type with a gradient or pattern if the type has not been converted to outlines. Find out how to make patterns in the "Patterns" technique on page 142 and create a dot pattern you can use as a shadow fill color.

Drop Shadow Filter

Illustrator also has its own Drop Shadow filter that you could use in place of Step 2. Do Step 1 to select the type. You must convert the type to outlines to use this filter. Then choose Filter➡Stylize➡Drop Shadow to open the Drop Shadow dialog box. The higher the Intensity setting (100%), the darker the shadow. Set the X and Y offset values (2.5 for both), click OK, and you're done.

 TIP To get the Drop Shadow filter to make a black shadow, simply set the Darker percentage to 100.

Transformation Tools

Use the transformation tools to simultaneously distort and copy type. This adds a little variation to the copy and paste technique.

1 To make this shadow, complete Step 1 and set the fill color to black (Stroke: none).

2 Select the Shear tool, select the type, and click once on the lower-left corner of the type to set the axis point for the Shear action.

199

Lurking

Lurking

Lurking

Deep

in the

3 After the crosshairs change into an arrow, click the pointer and drag it from the upper-right corner of the text to the right while holding down the Shift and (Option)[Alt] keys.

4 Choose a new fill color for the new, skewed copy.

VARIATION

Send the skewed copy to the back (Command-Shift-[)[Control-Shift-[ ] to make it the shadow.

In Step 2, select the Scale tool instead and set its axis point at the bottom center of the type. Drag from the upper-right toward the axis point while holding down the (Option)[Alt] key. Press (Command-Shift-[ )[Control-Shift-[ ] to send the shadow copy to the back. Set the fill color for both copies.

Try the Rotate tool. Select it in Step 2, and set its axis point at the bottom-center of the type. Click the pointer and drag it in a counter-clockwise or clockwise direction around the axis point while holding down the (Option)[Alt] key.

Finally, the Swirl tool. You must convert the type to outlines to use the Swirl tool. You also must copy the type, because the Swirl cannot create copies. In Step 2, select the Swirl tool, and click once to set the axis point in the center of the type. Click the pointer and drag it clockwise or counter-clockwise to swirl the type. Paste a copy of the original type in back for the shadow (Command-B)[Control-B], and set the fill color.

Floating Shadow

1 Enter the text, using the Type tool (Garton, 80 points). Choose Type➡Create Outlines, and set the fill and stroke colors for the type.

2 Select the Shear tool and click the lower-left corner of the type to set the Shear axis point. Click the pointer and drag it from the upper-right corner of the type toward the left. The type will lean to the left.

3 Select the Rotate tool. Again, click on the lower-left corner of the type to set the Rotate axis point. Click the arrow and drag it to rotate the type counter-clockwise just a little.

201

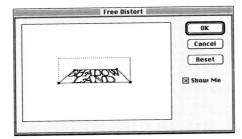

4 Select the Selection tool and hold down the (Option)[Alt] key while dragging the type down and a little to the left if you like. This copy will be the shadow. Set the fill color to black (or another color for the shadow), then press (Command-Shift-[)[Control-Shift-[ ] to send it to the back.

VARIATION

1 Complete Step 1 of Floating Shadow, then choose Filter➡ Distort➡Free Distort. Slide the two top corners together and down like this, then click OK to create this receding type.

2 Complete Step 4 of Floating shadow. ■

By expanding a gradient into individual paths, you can create type made of very fine lines.

1 Use the Type tool to enter the text. By the time you're through, the type will look quite a bit different, so don't worry too much about font selection. I used Gadzoox at 125 points (Tracking: 40). Choose Type➥Create Outlines.

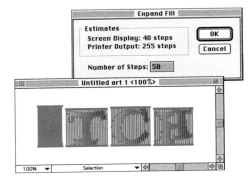

2 Set the fill color for the type to the Black, White preset gradient. Then choose Object➥Expand Fill. The greater the number entered into the Expand Fill dialog box, the finer the shaggy lines will be in the type. I set the steps at 50. There may be so many lines that you can't see the type.

3 Choose Object➥Masks➥ Release. The fill will spread outside the type outlines and the type will look like rectangles made of stripes.

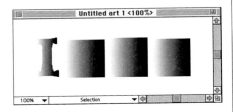

4 Use the Selection tool to select one letter at a time. Make sure that you select all of the stripes behind the type outlines as well as the type outlines themselves. Choose Object➥Pathfinder➥Crop. The letter should now be composed of very thin stripes, and everything else should disappear.

5 Do the same for each letter until they are all composed of thin stripes. Select all of the type and set the fill color (I used CMYK: 55, 45, 15, 40). Press (Command-Shift-G) [Control-Shift-G] to ungroup the lines that make up the type.

 You can press (Command-4) [Control-4] to repeat the Crop command, or any other Pathfinder command.

6 Select all of the type, and choose Filter➞Distort➞Scribble and Tweak. Choose the Scribble option. Set the Horizontal percentage to 10 and the Vertical percentage to between 10 and 20. The other settings will have little effect on the outcome.

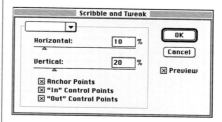

The type should look pretty shaggy now.

7 Use the Selection tool to select the first letter only (all of the lines that make the first letter).

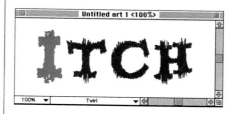

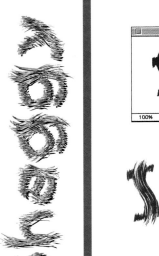

8 Select the Twirl tool. Click the tool (crosshairs) once in the center of the letter. Then click (the arrow) and drag it from the edge of the type around the center point. You will see the type twirl. Don't go too far, unless you're not concerned with readability.

9 Do the same for each letter. I rotated some letters clockwise and others counter-clockwise.

| TIP | **To exaggerate the frayed edges, select all of the letters and choose Filter➡ Distort➡Punk & Bloat. Use a negative (Punk) percentage—something near –20%.** |

VARIATIONS

If you want shagginess on the interior of the letters, click the Switch icon on the Tool palette to switch the fill and stroke colors. Setting the fill color to none will allow you to see through the type. Also set the stroke weight to 0.5 point.

For an even more transparent look, turn on the Dashed Line option. Set the first Dash to 12 and the first Gap to 16.

Choose Object➡Pathfinder➡
Exclude, then press (Command-
Shift-G)[Control-Shift-G] to
ungroup the pieces. Choose
Object➡Transform➡Transform
Each. Turn on the Random and
Preview options, and set the Rotate
angle to 350 to open up the type a
little.

I set the fill color for all pieces to a
copper gradient that I custom made.

To create this three-color, striped,
shaggy type, begin with the type
shown in the previous figure and
follow these steps. Use the Direct
Selection tool to drag a selection
rectangle across the middle of the
type. Then cut the selection, leaving
only the tops and bottoms of the
letters. Set the fill color for the top
pieces, then set the fill color for the
bottom pieces. Press (Command-A)
[Control-A], (Command-B)
[Control-B] to paste the middle
section in back of the top and bottom. Set the fill color for the middle section. For the thick outline,
select all of the pieces, copy, and
paste them in back. Set the stroke
color to black and set the stroke
weight to 4 points. ■

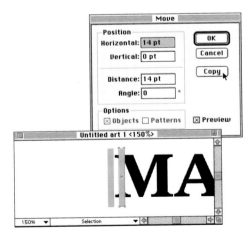

Here is a twist on the "Stripes" effect that uses the Transform Each filter to create some randomness.

1 Use the Type tool to enter the text. I tried Impulse at 75 points. Choose Type➡Create Outlines. Choose Object➡Compound Paths➡Make. Press (Command-L) [Control-L] to lock the type outlines. We'll come back to them later. For now, the type will serve as a guide for creating the stripes in the next few steps.

2 Use the Rectangle tool to make a thick, short (but taller than your type) stripe. To create the rectangle, click the Rectangle tool once in the image area. A dialog box will open. Set the Height to the same as the point size of the type (75 points). Adjust the Width so that about seven stripes can fit over a letter of normal width (7 points, in my case). It may take a few tries to find the right Width. Just press (Command-Z) [Control-Z] and repeat this step.

3 Move the rectangle to the left of the type as shown in the previous figure. Double-click the Selection tool to open the Move dialog box. Set the Horizontal move value to double the Width of the rectangle created in Step 1. Set the Vertical move value to 0, and click Copy.

4 Press (Command-D)[Control-D] as many times as it takes to create a row of spaced stripes that is longer than the type you will use. Set the stroke color to none and set the fill color to any color you want for one set of the stripes.

5 Select all of the stripes and double-click the Selection tool again to reopen the Move dialog box. Set the Horizontal move distance to the Width you used in Step 2. The Vertical move value should still be 0. Click Copy. Set the fill color to a different color for this new set of stripes. The type should now be hidden behind the rectangles.

6 Select all of the stripes, then double-click the Shear tool to open the Shear dialog box. Set the Angle to 15° and the axis to Horizontal. Click OK to slant the stripes.

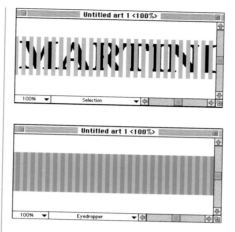

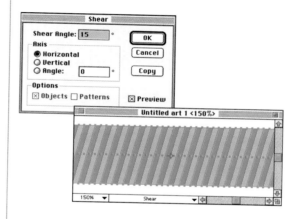

TIP If the typeface you are using has a slant to it, then you may want to skip Step 5. It is important that the angle of stripes does not line up with the angle of the type, which may occur with an italic or oblique font. You may also shear the stripes with a negative **Shear Angle** value to slant them in the opposite direction.

7 Press (Command-Shift-[ ) [Control-Shift-[ ] to send the stripes in back of the type. Press (Command-Shift-L)[Control-Shift-L] to unlock (and select) the type. Move the type or stripes, if necessary, to make sure that there are stripes behind all parts of the letters.

8 Select everything (type and stripes) and choose Object➧ Pathfinder➧Crop. The type has now been divided into stripes. Press (Command-Shift-G)[Control-Shift-G] to ungroup the stripes.

9 Select one of the stripes, and choose Edit➧Select➧Same Fill Color to select all of the stripes of that color. Use the arrow keys to displace this set of stripes up and to the left—2 keystrokes each.

10 Select all of the stripes (both colors), and choose Object➧ Transform➧Transform Each. Turn on the Random and Preview options. Bump the Horizontal and Vertical Move values up to about 3 points each. Click OK.

VARIATIONS

Add a Shadow

Select one of the stripes and choose Edit➡Select➡Same Fill Color. Copy the selected stripes, then paste them in back (Command-B)[Control-B]. Group the copied stripes (Command-G) [Control-G]. Set the fill color to black or another color for the shadow. Finally, use the arrow keys to shift the shadow away from the original (down one stroke, left one stroke).

More Colors

Instead of pasting the shadow copy in back, paste it in front (Command-F)[Control-F]. Set the fill color to none and set the stroke color to a new color (CMYK 12, 2, 70, 2). Set the stroke weight to .5 points. Choose Object➡Path➡Add Anchor Points. Repeat this step two more times to add even more points. Choose Filter➡Distort➡ Scribble and Tweak. Try these settings: Tweak, Horizontal: 1%, Vertical: 1%.

MARTINI

Transparent Layers

One color of stripes is in front of the other. Select one of the stripes in front. Then choose Edit→Select→Same Fill Color. Copy the stripes, then paste the copy in front (Command-F)[Control-F]. Use the arrow keys to shift the type in one direction or the other (two keystrokes up, two keystrokes left). Set the fill color of the new set of stripes to a color lighter than the other two colors. Select all three sets of stripes, and choose Object→Pathfinder→Soft. I left the Mixing Rate at the default: 50%.

Masked

Place an image and press (Command-Shift-[)[Control-Shift-[ ] to send the image to the back. Select one of the stripes. Choose Edit→Select→Same Fill Color. Press (Command-8) [Control-8] to turn the selected stripes into a single compound path. Select the new compound path and the placed image. Press (Command-7)[Control-7] to mask the image into the type.

Set the fill color of the other set of stripes to black. Then use the Selection tool to select the mask outlines. Copy, Select All, (Command-A)[Control-A] and paste them in back (Command-B) [Control-B]. Set their fill color also to black. Use the arrow keys to shift this new copy away from the originals (down two keystrokes, left two keystrokes). ■

Complex three-dimensional effects are probably best left to 3-D drawing applications, but Illustrator can perform some basic tasks that allow you to create the illusion that type is placed on a form.

Receding Flat Surfaces

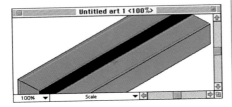

I Prepare a surface onto which you want the type to lay. I made this isometric box, but the surface does not need to be so exacting, read "anal." Select all of the background art and press (Command-L) [Control-L] to lock it.

2 Use the Type tool to enter the text. I used Blackletter686 at 120 points for this example. Make a good guess at the point size necessary for the surface. You can adjust the size later if you need to. Position the lower left-hand corner of the type at the approximate point it would be on the receding surface. Choose Type➡Create Outlines.

 There is actually no need to convert the type to outlines if you want to keep the text editable. All of the following transformations will still work, and you'll be able to correct typos. In Step 5, to scale the type, adjust the Horizontal and Vertical Scaling percentages found on the Character palette—very cool. Converting to outlines, however, allows you to do more with the type— filling it with gradients and patterns for example.

214

3 Select the Rotate tool and click the orientation point at the lower-left corner of the type. Then click near the end of the type and drag upward to rotate the type so that the baseline of the type is parallel with the bottom of the receding surface.

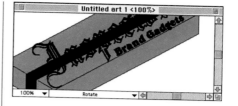

4 Select the Shear tool, and click the orientation point on the same lower-left corner of the type. Click the top-left corner of the type and then drag it away from the end of the type, along an imaginary line that runs along the surface that you're laying the type onto. This step should push the type down to lay on the surface.

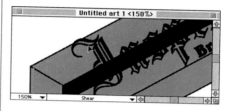

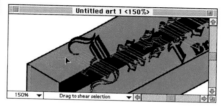

5 If desired or necessary, use the Scale tool to fit the type into the surface. Set the orientation point for the Scale tool at the same point as in the last two steps. Then click near the end of the type and drag the pointer toward the beginning of the type. Again, drag along an imaginary line parallel with the surface you're laying the type on. If you can't get the type to scale correctly, then undo back to Step 3, and scale the type before rotating it.

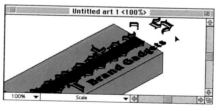

Color changes and a shadow
behind the brand name.

VARIATIONS

Isometric Planes

Three quick steps to putting type
on true isometric planes. Select the
type (Avenir) and set its Vertical
Scale at 86.6% on the Character
palette. Enter the following values
in the dialog boxes for the tools.
Double-click on each tool to access
its dialog box. 1) Shear: −30° (0°
Angle), Rotate: 30°; 2) Shear: 30°
(0° Angle), Rotate: 30°; 3) Shear:
−30° (0° Angle), Rotate: −30°.

Quick Perspective

I Enter the text using the Type tool
(BodegaSans BlackOldstyle, 100
points) and choose Type➡Create
Outlines, or select the type that
you want to distort. Choose
Filter➡Distort➡Free Distort.
Move the corner points to skew
the type. I dragged the two right
corners and moved them closer
together. I moved the two left corners apart and then moved the two
sides closer together.

2 This foreshortening is necessary to create the proper illusion.

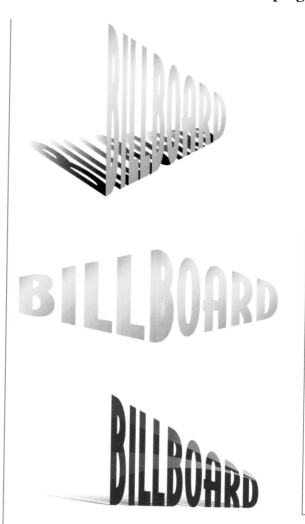

Corner Perspective

To put type on a corner select half of the type and distort it as above, then select the other half and distort it in the opposite direction. In this example, I cut the "B" so that part of it was selected to be on one side of the corner and the rest of it was selected to be on the other side.

The curving split in this text was created at the same time as the shaping. After converting the type into outlines, use the Pen tool to draw several diagonal lines across the type, then select the type and the lines and choose Object➡ Pathfinder➡Divide. Group the shapes within each tapered stripe so they will be easier to select later. Select all and choose Filter➡ Distort➡Free Distort. Distort the type as in Quick Perspective. Select the grouped stripes and fill them with gradients.

KPT Vector Distort

KPT Warp Frame and KPT Vector Distort are both great for shaping type onto surfaces. This type was manipulated with the Spherize function in KPT Vector Distort.

Vector Tools VectorShape

Extensis' VectorTools contains a VectorShape palette that enables you to map objects onto four different types of surfaces: spheres, cylinders, cones, and star. The Water, Waves, and Free distortion modes are also helpful for shaping type. Because VectorShape wraps the selected object to the edge of the shape, it is a good idea to create a larger box around the type when using this palette. Select the box with the type before applying the distortion. The box will keep the type away from the shapes edges where the distortion could be too great. Here is the VectorShape palette. ■

Use the Pen and Rotate tools to create a radial pattern that the Divide pathfinder can use to impact shatter your type.

1 Use the Type tool to enter the text. I used Impact at 100 points. Choose Type➡Create Outlines.

2 Use the Pen tool to draw a line from the center of the shatter impact to a short distance past one end of the type. Select the line.

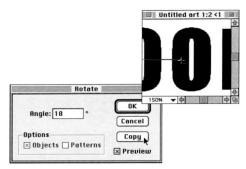

3 Select the Rotate tool. Hold down the (Option)[Alt] key and click on the beginning of the line (in the center of the type). The smaller the rotate angle you choose, the more pieces the type will be broken into. I set the Angle at 18°. Click Copy.

TOOLBOX

KPT Vector
Effects

4 Press (Command-D)[Control-D] to repeat the Rotate and copy. Keep pressing (Command-D) [Control-D] until the radius lines are copied into a full circle (18 times in my case). Don't worry about whether or not the spacing between the last radius and the original radius is different from the rest.

5 Select all of the radius lines and choose Object➡Transform➡ Transform Each. Turn on the Random and Preview options. Set the Rotate Angle to around 20°, or just enough to relieve the exact- ness of their placement.

6 Double-click the Reflect tool to display the Reflect dialog box, choose Vertical, and click Copy.

7 Double-click the Rotate tool to display the Rotate dialog box. Set the Rotate value to approximately one-half the value used in Step 3. Click OK. These last two Steps cre- ate a second set of radial lines that add variation to the shattered effect.

8 Select everything—all radius lines and type outlines. Choose Object➡ Pathfinder➡Divide. Press (Command-Shift-G)[Control-Shift- G] to ungroup the divisions.

9 Use the Selection tool to select one of the pieces inside the letters. Choose Edit➡Select➡Select Same Fill Color (none). Press Delete to remove all of the extra pieces.

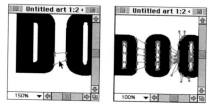

In this figure I chose Edit➡Select All to show all of the pieces that remained.

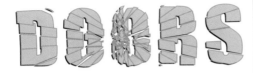

10 For clarity, this is a good time to change the color of the black pieces. I set the fill color to 50% Cyan, and set the stroke color to 100% Cyan.

11 Again, choose Object➧Transform➧Transform Each. Set the Horizontal and Vertical Move distances to low values. I set them both at 5. I also set the Rotate Angle to 5°. You can repeat this step to move things around a little more.

12 To create a shadow, select all of the pieces, copy and paste them in back (Command-B)[Control-B]. Shift them away from the type with the arrow keys. Then choose Object➧Transform➧Transform Each (Horizontal Move: 3 points, Vertical Move: 3 points, Rotate: 3°, Random). Click OK. Select the Twirl tool, then hold down the (Option) [Alt] key and click in the center of all of the pieces to open the Twirl dialog box. Set the Angle to 2°.

VARIATIONS

Before entering the text in Step 1, use the Rectangle tool to create a large rectangle. Set the fill color for the rectangle to any color except none. Center the type over the rectangle. After turning the type into outlines in Step 1, choose Object➧Compound Paths➧Make. Then select the rectangle and the type. Choose Object➧Pathfinder➧Minus Front. The type will be cut out of the rectangle, and everything will automatically become a single compound path.

Complete the rest of the steps. In Steps 2 through 4 make sure that the radius lines extend beyond the border of the rectangle.

KPT Shatterbox

After turning the type into outlines, KPT Shatterbox (Filter➡KPT Vector Effects➡KPT Shatterbox) can do all of this in one step (except the shadow). You can even create multiple impact points. Warning: keep the settings very low. ■

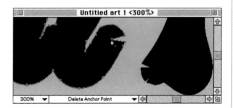

Pull up to the counter at Phil's and try this effect that's all about layering.

1 Enter the text using the Type tool. The typeface is crucial here. Choose a script font that is thick enough to hold up against a McDonald's sign. The best one I had on hand for this effect was Freehand 575 BT (150 points, Tracking: 25). Choose Type➡Create Outlines. The type should be black with no stroke. Press (Command-G) [Control-G] to group the type.

2 Choose Object➡Path➡Offset Path. Set the Offset to 8 points. The amount that you offset the type paths depends on the size of your type. Adjust the value as required to spread the type outlines outward. Set the Joins to Round. This filter will create some odd shapes inside the new, expanded type. Choose Object➡Pathfinder➡Unite to get rid of them. Set the fill color. I used CMYK: 12.5, 0, 25, 0. Press (Command-[)[Control-[ ] until all of the expanded type is behind the original (black) type.

TIP After offsetting the type, there may be some corners of the type that the offset filter did not fill in. **Zoom in to these areas and** use the Pen tool **to clean them up before moving on. Simply subtracting the interior corner point will fix the problem.**

3 Copy the expanded type and paste it in back (Command-B) [Control-B]. Set the fill color to black and use the arrow keys to offset the type down and to the right.

4 Copy the original type, the black type in front, and press (Command-F) [Control-F] to paste a copy in front. Set the fill color for this copy that will be the front of the type. I used the Green, Blue gradient.

5 Move the type up and to the left.

6 Copy the type and paste it in back (Command-B)[Control-B]. Move the copy down and to the right, and set the fill and stroke colors to the same color (I used CMYK: 0, 0, 100, 0). Set the stroke weight to 1 point.

7 Copy the type, then paste another copy in back (Command-B) [Control-B]. Set the stroke color to black and set the stroke weight to 2 points. This will create a very slight stroke around the yellow copy of the type.

8 Do any shifting around and color changes you need to make. ■

More fun from the Ink Pen filter! Use the Ink Pen filter to layer three colored copies of random swatches.

1 Use the Type tool to enter the text (I used Humanist521BT ExtraBold 95 points). Choose Type➡Create Outlines. Set the fill color for the type (CMYK: 40, 0, 85, 0). This color will be the color for the first set of spatters. Copy the type.

2 If you want the spatters to cover only part of the type, then use the Knife tool to cut off the type where you can contain the spatters. Select and delete the pieces of the letters that you do not want to get spattered. Group the pieces that remain. If you want the texture to fill all of the type, then paste a copy of the type in front (Command-F) [Control-F], set the fill color, skip Step 3, and ignore the "Select the cut type" in Step 4.

3 Paste a copy of the type in back (Command-B)[Control-B]. Set the fill color for the base of the type (CMYK: 0, 100, 100, 0).

4 Select the cut type, and press (Command-8)[Control-8] to turn the type into a single compound path. Copy the type. Then choose Filter→Ink Pen→Effects to open the Ink Pen dialog box. There are many settings to contend with in this dialog box. The settings here make a lot of sense and actually, believe it or not, produce predictable results. Watch the helpful, although tiny, Preview window as you make changes to the settings. First, click on the Hatch pop-up menu and choose the Swash hatch.

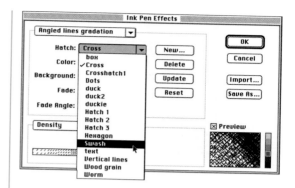

5 Set the Color to Match Object. The color chosen in Step 2 will be applied to the preset texture (Background: Hatch Only, Fade: None).

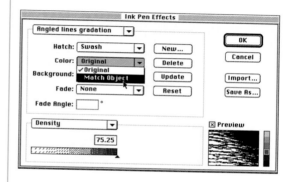

6 At the bottom of the dialog box is a pop-up menu that contains the titles of five more settings: Density, Dispersion, Thickness, Rotation and Scale. Choose each and use these settings: Density (43), Dispersion (Random; Range: 0, 97), Thickness (no settings), Rotation (Random; Range: –90°, 90°), Scale (Linear; Range: 10, 450; Angle: –90°).

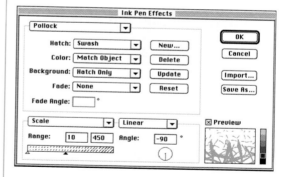

227

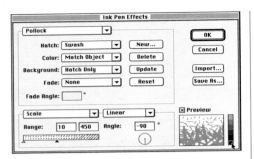

7 To the right of the Preview is a scale of gray swatches. These swatches further effect the density of the texture. Click on the bottom swatch to select a dense initial arrangement.

Click OK to see the texture applied to the type.

8 Press (Command-A)[Control-A] to select everything, then paste a copy of the type (the cut type if you used the Knife tool in Step 2) in front (Command-F)[Control-F]. Set the fill color of the type to a color for the second set of swashes (CMYK: 0, 35, 90, 0).

9 Press (Command-Option-E) [Control-Alt-E] to re-open the Ink Pen dialog box. Click on the third gray swatch to the right of the Preview window. Click OK to apply the filter again.

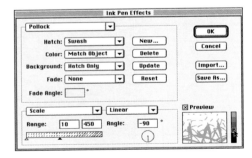

Now you can see what path I've been leading you down.

10 Repeat Steps 7 and 8. Select a new fill color in Step 7 (CMYK: 5, 5, 95, 0). In Step 8, select the first gray swatch beside the preview.

11 An offset shadow finishes the effect.

VARIATIONS

The following variations can be made by applying the Ink Pen once. Follow Step 1 (the fill color will be the color of the type) above. Paste a copy of the type in front (Command-F)[Control-F]. Choose Filter➡Ink Pen➡Effects, and use these settings in the Ink Pen dialog box:

Dalmatians

Hatch: Dots; Color: Original; Background: Hatch Only; Fade: None; Density (55); Dispersion (Random; Range: 100, 300); Thickness (no settings); Rotation (Random; Range: −71°, 62°); Scale (Random; Range: 500, 800). Choose the second gray swatch from the scale next to the Preview.

229

Soiled

Set the fill color of the type before choosing the Ink Pen filter. The fill color will become the color of the spots.

Hatch: Dots; Color: Match Object; Background: Hatch Only; Fade: None; Density (100); Dispersion (Random; Range: 100, 300); Thickness (no settings); Rotation (Random; Range: −71°, 62°); Scale (Random; Range: 100, 400). Choose the third gray swatch from the scale next to the Preview.

Dispersing

Set the fill color of the type before choosing the Ink Pen filter. The fill color will become the color of the dispersing dots.

Hatch: Dots; Color: Match Object; Background: Hatch Only; Fade: None; Density (100); Dispersion (Random; Range: 100, 300); Thickness (no settings); Rotation (Random; Range: −71°, 62°); Scale (Linear; Range: 50, 620; Angle: −90°). Choose the fifth gray swatch from the scale next to the Preview.

Pock Marks

Set the fill color of the type to the same color as the background (white in this example) before choosing the Ink Pen filter. The fill color will create the illusion of pock-marked type.

Hatch: Dots; Color: Match Object; Background: Hatch Only; Fade: None; Density (100); Dispersion (Random; Range: 100, 300); Thickness (no settings); Rotation (none); Scale (Random; Range: 150, 200). Choose the third gray swatch from the scale next to the Preview. ■

Set up the Divide pathfinder to cut your type into stripes, then experiment with an array of effects, first the basic technique for creating stripe effects, then a few pages to demonstrate some of the variety of effects you can achieve with this effect. For an alternate method for creating stripes see "Masked Stripes," (page 238).

Perfect Fit

1 This basic technique will create evenly spaced strips that are custom fit to your type. Use the Type tool to enter the text (Garton, 95 points). Choose Type➡Create Outlines.

2 You can make stripes in any direction. To begin I will make horizontal stripes. Use the Pen tool to draw a straight line across the top of the type. Hold down the Shift key while clicking the second point of the line to keep the line perfectly horizontal.

3 Select the entire line just drawn with the Selection tool. Drag the line downward while holding down the Shift and (Option)[Alt] keys to place a copy of the line at the baseline of the type.

4 Next, select both lines only. Then select the Blend tool. Click once on the left end of the top line, then once on the left end of the bottom line.

5 A dialog box will open. Subtract one from the desired number of stripes and enter that value for the Steps. Leave the other values alone. Click OK to create the intermediate lines.

6 Select all of the lines and letters. Choose Object➡Pathfinder➡ Divide. Your type should now look like this. Not much has changed, but some of the lines should have disappeared.

7 The Divide filter will automatically group the divisions. Press (Command-Shift-G)[Control-Shift-G] to ungroup the individual stripes. Then use the Selection tool to select only one of the empty shapes that were created between the letters.

8 Choose Edit➡Select➡Same Fill Color (none) to select all of these empty shapes. Press Delete to get rid of them.

233

9 Use the Selection tool to select each row. Set the fill colors as you proceed. Group (Command-G) [Control-G] each row so they will be easy to edit later.

JAILBIRD

10 Striped type. Adding stroke colors for the stripes is a nice touch.

Vertical

1 Vertical stripes can be made with the same method. This is how the type looked after Step 5 (Futura CondensedExtraBold, 110 points, Tracking: 50). In Step 5, I set the number of Steps to 12.

2 After Step 8, I selected all of the stripes and filled them with the Black & White gradient.

Diagonal

1 Again, the procedure is the same. Use the Pen tool to draw an initial diagonal line, then follow the rest of the steps. I set the number of Steps in Step 5 to 18. Here is the type after Step 5.

2 After Step 8, select all of the stripes and set the fill color to the Purple, Red, & Yellow gradient. Then select half of the stripes and change the Gradient angle (on the Gradient palette) to −180°.

Shifting

Any striped type made by the methods mentioned earlier, can be tweaked to shake up the type. Simply select all of the type and choose Object➡Transform➡ Transform Each. This dialog box will appear.

I used the settings in the previous figure, two different fills, and shadows to produce this type.

Floating

You can also float one row of stripes on top of another. Select all of one color of the stripes. Press (Command-Shift-])[Control-Shift-]] to send the stripes to the front. Copy the stripes, then press (Command-B)[Control-B] to paste the copy behind the originals. Set the fill color of the copies to black (or any color for a shadow). Use the arrow keys to shift the shadows away from the top stripes (Down Arrow key once, Left Arrow key once).

You could just delete the other set of stripes, and add more copies in back with varied fill and stroke settings.

Masked

Select one copy of the stripes, press (Command-8)[Control-8] to make them a single compound path. Place an image behind the stripes. Select the image and the stripes, (the compound path set only) and press choose Object→ Compound Paths→Make.

This type started a little simpler (shown here after Step 5).

235

RACING

Complete the steps as for the Perfect Fit effect. Select the middle shapes created by the two lines and press (Command-8)[Control-8] to make them a single compound path. Place an image behind the compound path. This image was created with KPT Gradient Designer in Photoshop. Select the image and the compound path. Choose Object→Compound Paths→Make.

> **TIP** After creating the mask, the image can still be shifted simply by selecting and dragging it.

Knocked Out

1 Create the stripes as boxes using the Rectangle tool. Fill them with two or more different colors. Select all stripes of one color and choose Object→Compound Paths→Make. Do the same for each color.

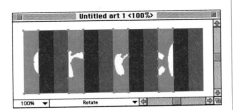

2 Place the type, converted to outlines, in front of the stripes. Select the type outlines and choose Object→Compound Paths→Make. Copy the type. Select one set of stripes and the type. Choose Object→Pathfinder→Minus Front. The type will knock out pieces from these stripes only.

3 Paste the type in front (Command-F)[Control-F]. Shift-select another set of stripes and press (Command-2)[Control-2] to repeat the Minus Front Pathfinder. Repeat this process for each set of stripes.

4 Select all and ungroup the cut-up stripes (Command-Shift-G) [Control-Shift-G]. Choose Object➤Transform➤Transform Each. Turn on the Random and Preview options. Bump the Rotate Angle up to about 28°. Click the Random option on and off to see different variations

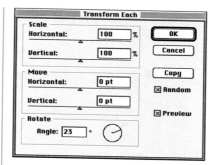

5 Select all, copy, paste in back (Command-B)[Control-B], and fill with 35% black to create a shadow. Shift the shadow away from the stripes. ■

In this method for creating striped text, the stripes are created first, and then the type outlines are used as a mask for the stripes. This method enables you to do more with the stripes, and it gives you greater flexibility for editing the stripes later. See the previous section, "Cut Stripes," for more techniques for creating stripes.

Swirl

1 Use the Rectangle tool to make a box like this and set the fill color.

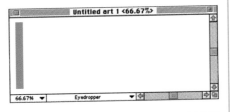

2 Use the Selection tool to select the box by clicking on its upper-left corner. Hold down the (Shift-Option)[Shift-Alt] keys and drag the box to the right until the pointer is directly on top of the upper-right corner of the original box. A copy has been made and it should be butted against the original. Set the fill color for the second box.

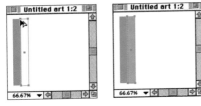

3 Select both boxes and hold the (Shift-Option)[Shift-Alt] keys as you drag them to the right until these copies butt against the originals.

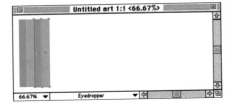

TOOLBOX

Extensis
VectorTools

4 Press (Command-D)[Control-D] to repeat the copy and move. Press (Command-D)[Control-D] as many times as it takes to create a row of stripes that can contain your type.

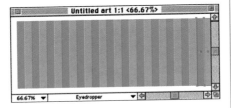

5 Select all of the stripes, and choose the Twirl tool from the Tools palette. Click once in the center of the stripes to set the center point for the Twirl tool. Then click outside the stripes and drag in a clockwise motion to twirl the stripes. When satisfied, release the mouse.

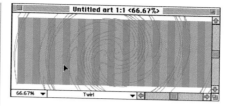

6 Next, use the Type tool to enter the text. I used Frutiger UltraBlack at 110 points. Choose Type➡ Create Outlines. While the type is still selected choose Object➡ Compound Paths➡Make. Copy the type. I also used the Scale tool to scale the swirl to fit my type.

7 Select everything and choose Objects➡Masks➡Make. I added a stroke and a shadow using the type copied in Step 6. Finally, I copied the swirling stripes to make a swirling background.

Stripes

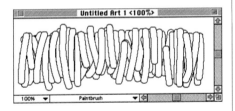

VARIATIONS

Using a mask to contain the stripes allows you to create any sort of stripe.

The Swoosh

A single swoosh. Double-click the Paintbrush tool to set the Width of the stroke (12 points). Click one stroke and drag it across the type. Choose Object➡Path➡Add Anchor Points. Repeat this four or five times to fill the path with points. Choose Filter➡Distort➡ Scribble and Tweak (Tweak, Horizontal: 16%, Vertical: 5%). Complete Steps 6 and 7 of "Swirl" to mask the swoosh into the type.

Painterly Stripes

Double-click the Paintbrush tool to set the options for painting (12 points). Use the Paintbrush to create an overlapping mess. Select all of the lines and choose Filter➡ Distort➡Roughen (Size: 5%, Detail: 60/in, Corner). Set varied fill colors or use VectorTools VectorColor to randomize the fill and stroke colors. Complete Steps 6 and 7.

Stripes Galore

Create a mess of stripes using the Rectangle tool. Select all of the stripes and choose Object➡ Transform➡Transform Each. Turn on the Random option and raise the Rotate Angle to about 30°. Complete Steps 6 and 7. Select the rectangles only and choose Filter➡ Distort➡Scribble and Tweak (Tweak, Horizontal: 30%, Vertical 5%). VectorTools VectorColor Randomize helped choose colors for this effect.

Glowing

1 Begin with a box created by using the Rectangle tool. Set the fill color to the Yellow to Purple radial gradient.

2 Use the Scale tool to stretch the box like this (600% Vertical only).

3 Draw another box over the first to cover the bottom half of the first box. Then select both and choose Object➡Pathfinder➡Minus Front. Deselect the box. Use the Direct Selection tool to click the top bar of the box, and drag it straight upwards to stretch the rectangle.

4 Make duplicates of the box as described in Step 2 of the "Swirl" technique (page 238).

5 Complete Steps 6 and 7 of "Swirl" to mask the text.

Radial

1 Use the Pen tool to draw a straight line that extends from the center of the image area outwards. This line is approximately 2-3/8 inches long.

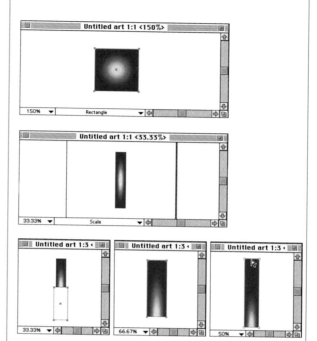
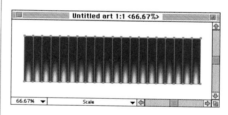

241

2 Select the line, then choose the Rotate tool. Hold down the (Option)[Alt] key and click on the original point of the line (in the center of the image area).

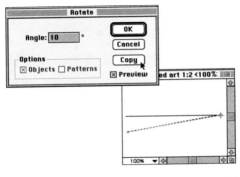

3 A dialog box will appear. Take 360° and divide it by the number of stripes you want in your type. I wanted 36 stripes, so I typed in 10° for the angle. Don't click OK—the original line will disappear. Instead, click Copy.

4 Use the Direct-Selection tool to select the two points that meet. Press (Command-J)[Control-J] to join these two points. If the Join dialog box opens, then click OK to join the two points as a Corner. If it doesn't open, then they have automatically joined. The two radial lines are now part of the same path. Set the fill color for this first stripe (CMYK: 8, 8, 63, 6).

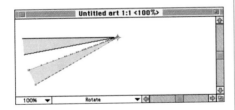

5 Next, use the Rotate tool again as you did in Step 2, except use a Rotation Angle that is exactly double the angle you used in Step 2. Click Copy. It should now appear as though there are two radial stripes separated by a gap that is equal to the width of the stripes.

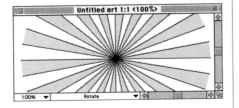

6 Press (Command-D)[Control-D] to repeat the Rotate command as many times as it takes to get around the circle. In this case 16 more times.

7 Next, select the Rectangle tool. Click the Rectangle tool in the center of the radial lines, hold the (Option)[Alt] key and drag outward toward the end of the radial lines. Draw the rectangle large enough to cover the type (to come later). Press (Command-Shift-[)[Control-Shift-[ ] to send the rectangle to the back. Set the fill color for the rectangle (CMYK: 15, 25, 80, 25).

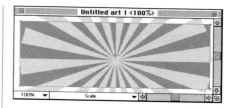

8 Complete Steps 6 and 7 of the "Swirl" method on page 239 to finish the effect. This is what you will have.

Jagged

1 Complete steps 1 through 4 of the "Swirl" method on page 238. Then select the Shear tool. With the lines selected, click on the bottom of the first line to set the axis of the Shear. Then hold down the Shift and (Option)[Alt] keys and click on the top of the next to last line. Drag from this point to the last point to make a sheared copy of the original.

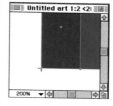 

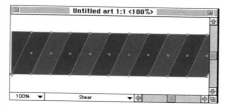

2 Select everything and choose Object➞Pathfinder➞Divide. Press (Command-Shift-G)[Control-Shift-G] to ungroup the stripes.

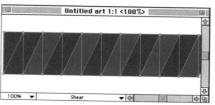

243

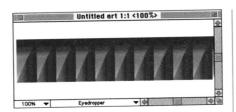

3 Next, select every other stripe and group them together. There should be two sets of stripes. One set looks like sails and the other set looks like, well, upside down sails. Set the fill color for each set to a different gradient.

4 Complete Steps 6 and 7 of the "Swirl" method on page 239. After masking the type, I selected the sails only and skewed them again. Simply double-click the Skew tool and click OK to repeat the Skew command with the last used settings.

Twisted

1 Complete Steps 1 and 2 of Jagged. Select the Twirl tool, click once in the center of the stripes, then click the pointer and drag it around the center to start the stripes twirling. Just put a little twirl in them.

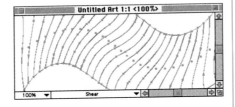

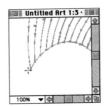

2 Select the Shear tool. Click once in the lower-left corner to set the anchor point for the skew. Then, while holding down the (Option) [Alt] key, click the pointer and drag it from the upper-right corner toward the right, just a bit. A slightly sheared copy of the twirled stripes is produced.

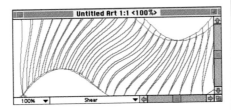

244

3 Complete Steps 2 through 4 of "Jagged." ■

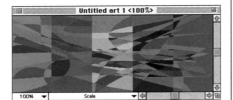

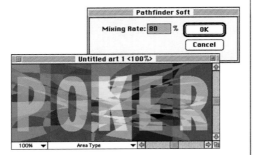

Illustrator cannot make truly transparent type like Photoshop can. However, you can use the Hard and Soft mixing filters to create the illusion of transparency.

1 Open a file containing an image or background that you want to place type over. This effect will not work on top of placed images. (See the Variations to find out how to fake the transparency over placed images.) The type must be on top of path objects—vector-based art. You could start with a few simple geometric shapes. I created this background using KPT Vector Effects Shatterbox.

2 Use the Type tool to enter the text. I used 135-point BodegaSans Black. Choose Type➡Create Outlines. Place the type over the background. Set the fill color to white, and copy the type.

3 Select the type and all of the pieces of the background that overlap the type. Choose Object➡Pathfinder➡Soft. This command will mix overlapping colors together. The higher the Mixing Rate the more the balance between the type color and the background color will lean toward the background color. I set the mixing rate at 80%. After the type and background have been mixed the type will be split into the areas defined by the background, so you will not be able to select the type easily.

4 However, because you copied the type in Step 2, you can paste it in front (Command-F)[Control-F], set the fill color to none, and set the stroke color to any color to give the type a stroke.

VARIATIONS

Transparent Shadows

Follow Steps 1 and 2, except set the fill color for the type to a darker color in Step 2. Results will be best if the color has some black in it. I used 50% gray and added 10% Cyan to add a little color to the shadow.

In Step 3, you have a choice. You can use the Soft pathfinder for a softer shadow, or try the Hard pathfinder as I did here.

Press (Command-F)[Control-F] to paste a copy of the type in front of the shadow. Use the arrow keys to shift the type away from the shadow. Set the fill and stroke colors as desired.

Transparent Perspective Shadows

Follow the same steps to create a transparent perspective shadow. See page 194 to find out how to distort the type outlines to create the receding shadow.

Add Gradients

After creating the shadow in the previous Variation, create gradients that start from the color created by the Hard (or Soft) pathfinder to the base color of the object underneath the shadow. You will need to create a gradient for each color of the background that the shadow runs over. Fill each piece of the shadow with the corresponding gradients. Select all of the shadow pieces, then select the Gradient tool and drag from the base of the type toward the end of the shadow.

Fake it on Placed Images

To fake transparent type on placed images, you need to have two copies of the image. In the application that created the background image (Photoshop in this case), create an altered version of the image. In Illustrator place the altered copy directly on top of the original placed image. Place the type on top of both. Select the type, after converting it to outlines, and the altered placed image. Choose Object➡Masks➡Make. ∎

Appendix A: Contributors Listing

Fonts

Delve Media Arts
P.O. Box 641053   (PC only)

San Francisco, CA 94164-1053

Phone: 415-474-0702

http://www.delvemediarts.com

delve@delvemediarts.com

Fonthead Design
1872-B Darryl Drive   (Mac and PC)

Tallahassee, FL 32301-6107

ethan@fonthead.com

http://www.fonthead.com

Foundry Group
Jon Armstrong   (Mac and PC)

c/o FondryGroup/Saiph Corporation

250 West 57th Street

New York, NY 10107

Phone: (718) 384-2583

jon@saiph.com

http://www.foundrygroup.com/

GarageFonts
P.O. Box 3101   (Mac and PC)

Del Mar, CA 92014

Phone: (619) 755-3913

Fax: (619) 755-4761

info@garagefonts.com

http://www.garagefonts.com/

Ingrimayne Type
Robert Schenk   (Mac and PC)

P.O. Box 404

Rensselaer, IN   47978

bobs@kagi.com

http://ingrimayne.saintjoe.edu/

Omnibus Typografi
Box 135   (Mac and PC)

S-135 23 Tyreso

Sweden

Phone: +46 8 742 8336

Fax: +46 8 712 3993

info@omnibus.se

http://www.omnibus.se

P22 Type Foundry
P.O. Box 770 West Side Station   (Mac and PC)

Buffalo, New York 14213-0070

Phone: (716) 885-4490

Fax: (716) 885-4482

p22@p22.com

http://www.p22.com

Ragnarok Press
P.O. Box 140333   (Mac only)

Austin, TX 78714

Phone: (512) 472-6535

Fax: (512) 472-6220

http://members.aol.com/ragnarokgc/scriptorium

Snyder Shareware Fonts
1797 Ross Inlet Road   (Mac and PC)

Coos Bay, OR 97420

snyderrp@mailF.coos.or.us

rps82@aol.com

76307.2431@compuserve.com

http://www.coos.or.ujs/~snyderp/

Synstelien Design
138 North 120th Plaza Apt. #9   (Mac and PC)

Omaha, NE 68154

Phone: (402) 491-3065

dsynstftrel@aol.com

http://www.synfonts.com

Three Islands Press
P.O. Box 442   (Mac and PC)

Rockland, ME 04841-0442

Phone: (207) 596-6768

Fax: (207) 596-7403

info@3ip.com

http://www.3ip.com/

Unleaded Type Foundry
Howard Bagley   (Mac and PC)

1208 M Street NW, Suite 6

Washington, D.C. 20005

Phone: (202) 737-2350

hbagley@worldnet.att.net

http://www.unleadedtype.com/

Vintage Type
5662 Calle Real #146   (Mac and PC)

Goleta, CA 93117-2317

sales@vintagetype.com

http://www.vintagetype.com/

Vitatype Digital Fonts
5204 Hadley Court, #1   (PC only)

Overland Park, KS 66202

Phone: (913) 677-2533

jeff@vitatype.com

http://www.primenet/~jeffib

Plug-in Demos

MetaTools, Inc.
6303 Carpinteria Ave.   KPT Vector Effects Demo (Mac only)

Carpinteria, CA 93013

(805) 566-6200

metasales@aol.com

http://www.metatools.com

Extensis Corporation
1800 SW 1st Street, Suite 500   Vector Tools 2.0 demo (Mac only)

Portland, OR 97201

Phone: (503) 274-2020

Fax: (503) 274-0530

sales@extensis.com

http://www.extensis.com

Alien Skin Software
1100 Wake Forest Road, Suite 101   Stylist demo (Mac only)

Raleigh, NC 27604

Phone: (919) 832-4124

Fax: (919) 832-4065

alienskinfo@alienskin.com

http://www.alienskin.com

Letraset USA
40 Eisenhower Drive   Envelopes demo (Mac only)

Paramus, NJ 07653

Phone: (800) 524-0785

Fax: (201) 909-2451

http:/www.letraset.com

Software

Adobe Systems, Inc.
345 Park Avenue   Acrobat Reader 3.0 (Mac and PC)

San Jose, CA 95110-6000   Photoshop 3.0.5 Tryout (Mac and PC)

Phone: (408) 536-6000   After Effects 3.0 Tryout (Mac only)

Fax: (408) 537-6000   Streamline 3.1 Tryout (Mac and PC)

sales@adobe.com   Dimensions 2.0 Tryout (Mac only)

http://www.adobe.com   Illustrator 6.0 Tryout (Mac only)

Macromedia
600 Townshend   Fotographer demo (Mac and PC)

San Francisco, CA 94103

Phone: (415) 252-2000

http://www.macromedia.com

Stock Images

253

Photo24 Texture Resource
7948 Faust Ave.

West Hills, CA 91304

Phone: (818) 999-4184 or (800) 582-9492 (outside CA)

Fax: (818) 999-5704

http://www.photo24.com

D'Pix Division of Amber Productions, Inc.
41 W. Fourth Ave.

Columbus, OH 43201

Phone: (614) 299-7192

Fax: (614) 294-0002

Appendix B: What's on the CD-ROM

The CD-ROM packaged with this book is full of things to help you to get the most out of Illustrator. It is both Macintosh and Windows compatible. There are, however, some resources that are not available for both platforms.

Included on the CD-ROM are more than 40 fonts, plug-in and software demos, and two collections of stock photography. Following are a few notes on using and accessing these files. More information on these files is located in the ReadMe files on the CD-ROM. It is suggested that you read them before installing the files.

Type Images

Peaking over someone's shoulder is a great way to learn. You can do that in a not so virtual way by examining the actual files of the type images that appear in this book. On the CD-ROM there is one example for each type effect in the book. All of these files are images that appear on the pages, but not everything that's in the book is on the CD-ROM. Looking at the images onscreen allows you to take a closer look than what you can see in the book. To open these files press (Command-O)[Control-O] and follow this path: Illustrator Type Magic➡ITM Files➡Effects. All files are saved in Illustrator 6.0 format, and can be accessed by Illustrator versions 6.0 and 7.0.

Fonts

This book shows you how to create the effects, but they all must begin with a typeface. Sometimes the typeface will make all of the difference in the effect. On the CD-ROM, 16 type foundries have provided fonts as samples of their collections.

Three types of fonts appear on the CD-ROM: Shareware, Freeware, and Licensed. Freeware fonts are free for you to use and distribute. Use of Shareware fonts obligates you to send the font developer or author a small fee.

Licensed fonts are provided on the CD-ROM for use by the purchaser of this book only. These are fonts that would normally be offered for sale by the developers and are not to be distributed. By using these fonts you enter in an agreement with the developer to follow these guidelines, as well as, those guidelines detailed in the ReadMe files associated with each font.

Respecting these guidelines ensures that these developers are able to continue producing these great fonts. Please consult the ReadMe files associated with each font foundry on the CD-ROM for more information on the use of particular fonts.

Both TrueType and PostScript font formats have been included when available. To install a font, choose which format you want to use, then follow the instructions in the next section.

Macintosh Users
Method 1:

Quit all running applications. Drag the fonts from the CD-ROM onto the Fonts folder located in the System Folder on your hard drive. The fonts will be available to all applications started after installing the fonts.

Method 2:

If you are using a font management utility such as Suitcase, then drag the fonts from the CD-ROM into the folder on your hard drive in which you keep your fonts. Use your font management software to access the fonts.

Windows Users
Fonts should be installed by means of the Fonts Control Panel. Under Windows 95 or Windows NT 4.0 open Start Menu➡Settings➡Control Panel➡Fonts. Then select File➡Install New Font... from the File Menu and select the font from the CD-ROM that you want to install. The fonts can all be found within the Fonts directory on the CD-ROM.

Software Demos
Demo versions of some of the most popular graphics programs are included on the CD-ROM. To tryout any of these applications, simply open its folder and double-click the Install icon.

Stock Photos
You may think of Photoshop when you think of using stock images, but as demonstrated in this book they can be very useful in Illustrator as well. Use them to fill type with a texture (see "Masked," page 104), or apply Photoshop filters to them directly within Illustrator (see "Rasterized," page 162). To place any of these files in an Illustrator document, choose File➡Place. Follow this path to find the stock images on the CD-ROM: Illustrator Type Magic➡Stock Images. Continue to move through the folders until you find a suitable image for your purpose. Click OK to place the image in Illustrator.

Plug-in Demos
Illustrator plug-ins have become very powerful. On the CD-ROM there are demo versions of the most popular plug-ins. These tools greatly enhance Illustrator's capabilities and will become key members of your everyday Illustrator command arsenal. To access the demos you will need to install them on your hard drive. Within the folder for each demo is a ReadMe file to walk you through the installation procedure. If there is no ReadMe file, then the plug-in contains an automatic installer. Double-click the installer to install the plug-in.

Gallery

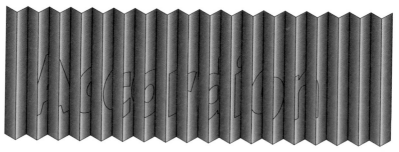

page 20

page 24

page 26

page 30

page 34

page 38

Dashed Outlines

page 42

page 48

page 54

page 58

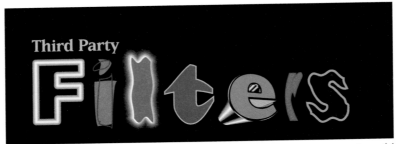

page 64

page 70

page 76

page 84

page 90

Overlapped

In Paths

On Paths

Path

Patterns

page 134

page 142

page 152

Photoshop

page 172

page 176

page 182

page 186

page 194

page 198

page 204

page 208

page 214

page 220

page 224

page 226

page 232

page 238

page 246

Illustrator Type Magic

Other DESIGN/GRAPHICS Titles

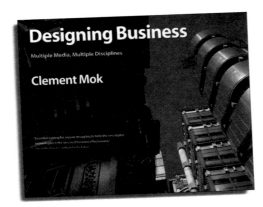

Designing Business

Multiple Media, Multiple Disciplines

Clement Mok

Designing Business

Provides the design/business communities with a new way of thinking about how the right design can be a strategic business advantage. It is the definitive guide to presenting a business identity through the use of traditional media vehicles and emerging technologies.

- CD-ROM (dual-platform) exhibits interactive prototypes of multimedia brochures, interactive television, and Web sites as developed by Clement Mok Designs Inc., one of the most sought after interactive design agencies in the world
- Shows how effective communication is one way to out-think, out-plan, and out-perform the competition

Clement Mok
1-56830-282-7 ■ $60.00 USA/$81.95 CDN
264 pp., 8 x 10, Covers PC and Macintosh, New - Expert
Available Now

Adobe Persuasion: Classroom in a Book
1-56830-316-5 ■ $40.00 USA/$56.95 CDN
Available November 1996

Learning Adobe FrameMaker
1-56830-290-8 ■ $60.00 USA/$81.95 CDN
Available Now

Adobe Illustrator for Windows: Classroom in a Book
1-56830-053-0 ■ $44.95 USA/$59.99 CDN
Available Now

Adobe PageMaker for Windows: Classroom in a Book
1-56830-184-7 ■ $45.00 USA/$61.95 CDN
Available Now

Adobe Photoshop: Classroom in a Book
1-56830-317-3 ■ $45.00 USA/$63.95 CDN
Available Now

Advanced Adobe PageMaker for Windows 95: Classroom in a Book
1-56830-262-2 ■ $50.00 USA/$68.95 CDN
Available Now

Advanced Adobe Photoshop for Windows: Classroom in a Book
1-56830-116-2 ■ $50.00 USA/$68.95 CDN
Available Now

The Amazing PhotoDeluxe Book for Windows
1-56830-286-X ■ $30.00 USA/$40.95 CDN
Available Now

Branding with Type
1-56830-248-7 ■ $18.00 USA/$24.95 CDN
Available Now

Digital Type Design Guide
1-56830-190-1 ■ $45.00 USA/$61.95 CDN
Available Now

Fractal Design Painter Creative Techniques
1-56830-283-5 ■ $45.00 USA/$56.95 CDN
Available Now

Photoshop 4 Type Magic 1
1-56830-380-7 ■ $39.99 USA/$47.95 CDN
Available Now

Photoshop Web Magic
1-56830-314-9 ■ $45.00 USA/$63.95 CDN
Available Now

Adobe Photoshop Complete
1-56830-323-8 ■ $49.99 USA/$61.95 CDN
Available Now

Stop Stealing Sheep & find out how type works
0-672-48543-5 ■ $19.95 USA/$26.99 CDN
Available Now

Visit your fine local bookstore, or for more information visit us at http//:www.mcp.com/hayden/

Other INTERNET Titles

Creating Killer Web Sites

The book has an accompanying Web site, where visitors can see the pages in action, download the code for their favorite designs, see tutorials and examples not found in the book, and interact with the author. An estimated 100,000 Web site designers are hungry for this information; by August of 1996, their number was expected to double.

- Conferences about designing for the Internet are selling out, and designers are challenged as they make the transition from print to new media design
- Written by one of today's most noted Web designers
- The first book to teach the art as well as the craft of site design

David Siegel
1-56830-289-4 ■ $45.00 USA/$63.95 CDN
272 pp., 8 x 10, Covers PC and Macintosh, Accomplished - Expert
Available Now

Macromedia Shockwave for Director
1-56830-275-4 ■ $30.00 USA/$40.95 CDN
Available Now

Photoshop Web Magic
1-56830-314-9 ■ $45.00 USA/$63.95 CDN
Available November 1996

Virtus VRML Toolkit
1-56830-247-9 ■ $40.00 USA/$54.95 CDN
Available Now

Designer's Guide to the Internet
1-56830-229-0 ■ $30.00 USA/$40.95 CDN
Available Now

Internet Starter Kit for Windows 95
1-56830-260-6 ■ $35.00 USA/$47.95 CDN
Available Now

Internet Starter Kit for Windows, Second Edition
1-56830-177-4 ■ $30.00 USA/$40.95 CDN
Available Now

The Adobe PageMill 2.0 Handbook
1-56830-313-0 ■ $39.99 USA/$56.95 CDN
Available Now

Designing Multimedia Web Sites
1-56830-308-4 ■ $50.00 USA/$70.95 CDN
Available Now

Designing Interactive Web Sites
1-56830-311-4 ■ $45.00 USA/$70.95 CDN
Available Now

Internet Publishing with Adobe Acrobat
1-56830-300-9 ■ $40.00 USA/$56.95 CDN
Available Now

Kids do the Web
1-56830-315-7 ■ $25.00 USA/$35.95 CDN
Available Now

Web Designer's Guide to Style Sheets
1-56830-306-8 ■ $39.99 USA/$49.95 CDN
Available Now

Web Page Scripting Techniques: JavaScript, VBScript, and Advanced HTML
1-56830-307-6 ■ $50.00 USA/$70.95 CDN
Available Now

World Wide Web Design Guide
1-56830-171-5 ■ $40.00 USA/$54.95 CDN
Available Now

Adobe PageMill 2.0: Classroom in a Book
1-56830-319-X ■ $40.00 USA/$56.95 CDN
Available Now

Visit your fine local bookstore, or for more information visit us at http//:www.mcp.com/hayden/

REGISTRATION CARD

Illustrator Type Magic

Hayden Books

Name _____ Title _____

Company_____Type of business _____

Address _____

City/State/ZIP _____

Have you used these types of books before? ☐ yes ☐ no

If yes, which ones? _____
_____

How many computer books do you purchase each year? ☐ 1–5 ☐ 6 or more

How did you learn about this book? _____

☐ recommended by a friend   ☐ received ad in mail
☐ recommended by store personnel ☐ read book review
☐ saw in catalog   ☐ saw on bookshelf

Where did you purchase this book? _____

Which applications do you currently use? _____

Which computer magazines do you subscribe to? _____

What trade shows do you attend? _____

Please number the top three factors which most influenced your decision for this book purchase.

☐ cover   ☐ price
☐ approach to content ☐ author's reputation
☐ logo   ☐ publisher's reputation
☐ layout/design   ☐ other _____

Would you like to be placed on our preferred mailing list? ☐ yes ☐ no email address _____

☐ **I would like to see my name in print!** You may use my name and quote me in future Hayden products and promotions. My daytime phone number is: _____

Comments _____
_____
_____

Hayden Books   Attn: Product Marketing ◆ 201 West 103rd Street ◆ Indianapolis, Indiana 46290 USA

Fax to **317-581-3576**   Visit our Web Page **http://www.mcp.com/hayden/**

Fold Here

BUSINESS REPLY MAIL
FIRST-CLASS MAIL PERMIT NO. 9918 INDIANAPOLIS IN

POSTAGE WILL BE PAID BY THE ADDRESSEE

HAYDEN BOOKS
Attn: Product Marketing
201 W 103RD ST
INDIANAPOLIS IN 46290-9058

PLUG YOURSELF INTO...

THE MACMILLAN
INFORMATION SUPERLIBRARY™

Free information and vast computer resources from the world's leading computer book publisher—online!

FIND THE BOOKS THAT ARE RIGHT FOR YOU!
A complete online catalog, plus sample chapters and tables of contents!

- **STAY INFORMED** with the latest computer industry news through our online newsletter, press releases, and customized Information SuperLibrary Reports.

- **GET FAST ANSWERS** to your questions about Hayden books.

- **VISIT** our online bookstore for the latest information and editions!

- **COMMUNICATE** with our expert authors through email and conferences.

- **DOWNLOAD SOFTWARE** from the immence Macmillan Computer Publishing library:
  - Source code, shareware, freeware, and demos.

- **DISCOVER HOT SPOTS** on other parts of the Internet.

- **WIN BOOKS** in ongoing contests and giveaways!

TO PLUG INTO HAYDEN:

WORLD WIDE WEB: **http://www.mcp.com/hayden/**

FTP: ftp.mcp.com

WANT MORE INFORMATION?

CHECK OUT THESE RELATED TOPICS OR SEE YOUR LOCAL BOOKSTORE

Adobe Press

Published by Hayden Books, the Adobe Press Library reveals the art and technology of communication. Designed and written by designers for designers, best-selling titles include the Classroom in a Book (CIAB) series for both *Macintosh* and *Windows* (*Adobe Photoshop CIAB, Advanced Adobe Photoshop CIAB, Adobe PageMaker CIAB, Advanced Adobe PageMaker CIAB, Adobe Illustrator CIAB,* and *Adobe Premiere CIAB*), the Professional Studio Techniques series (*Production Essentials, Imaging Essentials,* and *Design Essentials, 2E*), and *Interactivity by Design.*

Design and Desktop Publishing

Hayden Books is expanding its reach to the design market by publishing its own mix of cutting-edge titles for designers, artists, and desktop publishers. With many more to come, these must-have books include *Designer's Guide to the Internet, Adobe Illustrator Creative Techniques, Digital Type Design Guide,* and *The Complete Guide to Trapping, 2E.*

Internet and Communications

By answering the questions of what the Internet is, how you get connected, and how you can use it, *Internet Starter Kit for Macintosh* (now in 3rd Ed.) and *Internet Starter Kit for Windows* (now in 2nd Ed.) have proven to be Hayden's most successful titles ever, with over 500,000 Starter Kits in print. Hayden continues to be in the forefront by meeting your ever-popular demand for more Internet information with additional titles, including *Simply Amazing Internet for Macintosh, Create Your Own Home Page for Macintosh, Publishing on the World Wide Web, World Wide Web Design Guide, World Wide Web Starter Kit, net.speak: The Internet Dictionary,* and *Get on the Internet in 5 Minutes for Windows and Macintosh.*

Multimedia

As you embrace new technology's shaping of multimedia, Hayden Books will be publishing titles that help you understand and create your own multimedia projects. Books written for a wide range of audience levels include *Multimedia Starter Kit for Macintosh, 3D Starter Kit for Macintosh, QuickTime: The Official Guide for Macintosh Users, Virtual Playhouse, Macromedia Director Design Guide,* and *Macromedia Director Lingo Workshop.*

High-Tech

Hayden Books addresses your need for advanced technology tutorials and references by publishing the most comprehensive and dynamic titles possible, including *Programming Starter Kit for Macintosh, Tricks of the Mac Game Programming Gurus, Power Macintosh Programming Starter Kit, FoxPro Machete: Hacking FoxPro for Macintosh, 2E,* and *The Tao of AppleScript: BMUG's Guide to Macintosh Scripting, 2E.*

Orders/Customer Service   `800-763-7438`   **Source Code**   `HAYB`

Hayden Books   201 West 103rd Street ◆ Indianapolis, Indiana 46290 USA

Visit our Web page at `http://www.mcp.com/hayden/`

MACMILLAN COMPUTER PUBLISHING USA

A VIACOM COMPANY

Technical ---- Support:

If you cannot get the CD/Disk to install properly, or you need assistance with a particular situation in the book, please feel free to check out the Knowledge Base on our Web site at **http://www.superlibrary.com/general/support**. We have answers to our most Frequently Asked Questions listed there. If you do not find your specific question answered, please contact Macmillan Technical Support at **(317) 581-3833**. We can also be reached by email at **support@mcp.com**.